Sartre, Existentialism, and the New Age of Nausea

Stuart Sim

Sartre, Existentialism, and the New Age of Nausea

palgrave
macmillan

Stuart Sim
English and Creative Writing
Northumbria University (retired)
Newcastle upon Tyne, UK

ISBN 978-3-031-90773-9   ISBN 978-3-031-90774-6 (eBook)
https://doi.org/10.1007/978-3-031-90774-6

© The Editor(s) (if applicable) and The Author(s), under exclusive license to Springer Nature Switzerland AG 2025

This work is subject to copyright. All rights are solely and exclusively licensed by the Publisher, whether the whole or part of the material is concerned, specifically the rights of translation, reprinting, reuse of illustrations, recitation, broadcasting, reproduction on microfilms or in any other physical way, and transmission or information storage and retrieval, electronic adaptation, computer software, or by similar or dissimilar methodology now known or hereafter developed.
The use of general descriptive names, registered names, trademarks, service marks, etc. in this publication does not imply, even in the absence of a specific statement, that such names are exempt from the relevant protective laws and regulations and therefore free for general use.
The publisher, the authors and the editors are safe to assume that the advice and information in this book are believed to be true and accurate at the date of publication. Neither the publisher nor the authors or the editors give a warranty, expressed or implied, with respect to the material contained herein or for any errors or omissions that may have been made. The publisher remains neutral with regard to jurisdictional claims in published maps and institutional affiliations.

This Palgrave Macmillan imprint is published by the registered company Springer Nature Switzerland AG.
The registered company address is: Gewerbestrasse 11, 6330 Cham, Switzerland

If disposing of this product, please recycle the paper.

Acknowledgements

Thanks go to my editors at Palgrave for all their work in helping me get this project into shape, and to the readers of both the proposal and the eventual manuscript for their invariably sound advice as to how to improve it. As ever, special thanks are due to my wife, Dr. Helene Brandon, for listening to me going on about the project (often at great length, apologies) over the course of the writing period, and persuading me that it was worth persevering with.

Contents

1 Introduction: Fellow-Travelling with Jean-Paul Sartre   1

2 Political Authoritarianism   19

3 Climate Crisis   37

4 Universal Theories   53

5 A Somewhat Despairing Conclusion on Human Weakness   69

Index   87

CHAPTER 1

Introduction: Fellow-Travelling with Jean-Paul Sartre

Abstract The objective of this introductory chapter is to demonstrate the increasing relevance of Jean-Paul Sartre's existentialist philosophy to the contemporary socio-political landscape. The focus will be on Sartre's early novel *Nausea*, which will be utilised to address pressing issues in our culture such as political authoritarianism, climate change, and the uncritical belief that lies behind these fuelling conspiracy theories as it goes. That the growing influence wielded by the far right represents a major threat to Western democracy will be a central theme overall, and nausea seems an entirely appropriate reaction to this very worrying development. Sartre's main philosophical concepts, such as bad faith and authenticity (as outlined in works such as *Being and Nothingness*), will constitute a major point of reference for the book's arguments, and he will be identified as a fellow-traveller for our troubled times.

Keywords Jean-Paul Sartre • Existentialism • *Nausea* • Bad faith • Authenticity • Democracy • Climate change • Authoritarianism • Conspiracy theory

> 'Things are bad! Things are very bad: I've got it, that filthy thing, the Nausea'.[1]

A newspaper editorial recently referred to Blaise Pascal as a 'fellow-traveller' for our times, claiming that his thought still had considerable relevance to us several centuries on.[2] It is a point that can be made of a wide range of thinkers drawn from the Western philosophical tradition, whose theories continue to be applicable to addressing the major social and political issues of our culture in giving us valuable insights into how to deal with these. Karl Marx may be far less important now than he has been, but he is an outstanding example none the less of how philosophy can be turned to account in that manner by committed adherents (for good or ill depending on your ideological persuasion in this instance). I have deployed the work of the poststructuralist thinker Jean-François Lyotard to similar effect on several occasions over the past few years, and he will appear again at several points in this study.[3] What I want to argue here is that a particularly compelling case can also be made in that respect for Jean-Paul Sartre and the philosophy of existentialism that he developed. In an era where political authoritarianism has asserted itself so powerfully, and malignantly, internationally and where climate change has revealed the shortcomings of the political class so sharply, existentialism has much to offer as a worldview and source of ideas. The sense of a world order falling apart as crises multiply connects us strongly to Sartre's situation in the Europe of the 1930s and 1940s, when fascism was doing its utmost to dominate the political scene and human rights were under severe pressure as a direct result. Sartre responded with such works as his novel *Nausea*, which resonates only too meaningfully in the current socio-political climate to anyone positioned on the liberal democratic or social democratic scale—the more so the more left-wing one considers oneself to be. In both cases we are confronted by what can be called the 'politics of prejudice', with the far right concentrating on arousing our very worst instincts, as in their cynical campaign against 'woke' attitudes (basically, a belief in social justice and in having a social conscience, although you would not suspect that from listening to the far right, who make it sound like an attack on personal freedom prosecuted by the self-proclaimed politically correct). *Nausea* alone would make Sartre a fellow-traveller therefore, his later fiction and large-scale philosophical projects building on this designation.

Commentators on existentialism often remark on the difficulty of pinning down exactly what the term means, but Sarah Bakewell has usefully summed it up as a philosophy where the main focus is on '*individual, concrete human existence*'.[4] Sartre's main influences are to be found in phenomenology, as in the work of Edmund Husserl and, particularly, Martin Heidegger, philosophers similarly concerned with the nature of being. For Sartre 'existence precedes essence', by which he means 'that man first of all exists, encounters himself, surges up in the world – and defines himself afterwards'.[5] Each individual is free therefore to makes choices, and those choices will define what they become. The goal is to be authentic, facing up to reality as it is rather than deceiving ourselves as to its true nature, which would be bad faith on our part. Sartre rejects both religion and determinism of any kind, arguing that '[m]an is nothing else but that which he makes of himself' and has to take responsibility for that process and the effect it will have on others.[6] One can see how important the politics of the world around us would be on our development in that case.

Existentialism readily lends itself to such concerns and that has always constituted a significant part of its appeal. Sartre himself was politically very active throughout his life, being instrumental in founding, and then editing, the influential journal *Les Temps Modernes*, for example. This is a philosophy designed to deal with the everyday world, rather than with metaphysical abstractions of the kind that we find in theories such as Marxism and the tradition of dialectical philosophy behind it. Aside from his philosophical writings Sartre was also a novelist and dramatist of note, and as those fictional works have themes relating to his philosophy (very much so when it comes to *Nausea*) that helped to give existentialism much wider public exposure.

My intention is to demonstrate the relevance of Sartrean existentialism to the contemporary socio-political landscape and a specific set of problems that is emerging from this and causing considerable unease. This will involve looking at Sartre's fiction, with particular reference to *Nausea*, as well as the *Roads to Freedom* trilogy that followed it, in terms of how they can be utilised to address issues such as political authoritarianism, climate change and the uncritical belief that lies behind these fuelling conspiracy theories in its turn.[7] *Being and Nothingness*, where Sartre's main philosophical concepts are outlined in his version of phenomenology, will also be a major point of reference for the book's arguments.[8] I will be arguing that the worldview this body of work promotes remains very much valid for turbulent times such as our own. Sartre will be read through these, emphasising the renewed importance of the concepts of absurdity and authenticity to the contemporary geopolitical situation, where we find bad faith in the ascendant across both our political and corporate culture, distorting public debate and adversely affecting the response to the many crises we are facing on an increasingly frequent basis. Writing these off as mere 'wokeness' constitutes a crude attempt by the far right to divert attention away from how they are exploiting such situations to their own advantage—a theme I will keep returning to throughout the book. My aim will be to situate Sartre within our current geopolitical condition and its complex set of clashing ideologies to see where his thought can lead in making sense of it. And we really do need to get a grip on the rise of the far right before it swamps the democratic way of life entirely, as it is currently striving so hard to do. Bigotry is very obviously on the rise and its impact on public life cannot be allowed to go unchecked. We are living in an era, after all, when a prominent British right-wing politician can claim that ex-colonies should feel 'a debt of gratitude' to the UK for introducing them to Western values—civil rights, democracy, capitalism, etc.—and thus, according to Robert Jenrick, improving their overall quality of life.[9] Not that democracy and civil rights were what most of them experienced while under direct empire rule, but politicians can be very selective about historical facts when it suits their purposes, and the farther right they are on the spectrum then the more that will turn out to be the case. There will be more examples of this failing to note as we proceed.

Matthew C. Ally has sparked interest in existentialism's implications for environmental matters in his book *Ecology and Existence: Bringing Sartre to the Water's Edge*, and more recently the edited collection *Earthly Engagements: Reading Sartre After the Holocene*.[10] These raise the kind of issues I want to consider here, with *Earthly Engagements* setting out to answer the question Ronald Aronson poses in its Foreword: 'Is it outlandish to hope that a thinker born well over a century ago can help us understand and combat today's nightmares, born of the Anthropocene?'.[11] His response is that 'Sartre rises anew at the dawn of the Anthropocene, as we are forced to face our climate crisis'.[12] That is a sentiment I would endorse, and I will be expanding the list of issues Sartre can help us combat as much as possible in the study that follows. Philosophies and philosophers move in and out of fashion over the years, and I really do believe, with Ally and his cast of contributors, that Sartre and existentialism are coming into their own again. Even since 2023 when *Earthly Engagements* came out (and the writing would have predated that by a year or two, of course), the situation regarding climate crisis has become markedly more serious, as it has with another of my main topics, political authoritarianism (not to mention the conspiracy theory that comes in its wake). The updating that one of *Earthly Engagement*'s articles (originally published in 1991) engages in to prove the continuing validity of Sartre's thought, plainly needs to be taken much further, more than another thirty years down the line.[13] Existentialist thought has much to offer us right now, when we need all the intellectual help we can get.

Existentialist Times

Existentialist philosophy is very much the product of its times. It was developed in the Europe of the inter-war period when political totalitarianism—in the guise of both fascism and communism—was becoming ever more dominant, and Western society was struggling with the economic hardship brought on by the Great Depression. The attendant political and social tensions culminated in World War II and the Holocaust, to be followed by the Cold War, with the fear of nuclear war always there in the background (as it remains today to some extent, since nuclear stockpiles still exist in several countries, not all of whose leaders can be trusted to show restraint in this area). It was a time of considerable social and political turmoil, therefore, which had a profound, often disorienting, effect on all those caught up in it: the 'nausea' that Sartre's protagonist, Antoine Roquentin, so regularly experiences in the novel of that name capturing the sense of alienation and powerlessness that so many individuals undeniably, and entirely understandably, felt. Roquentin's plight is in the first place a philosophical one, and he is acting out several of the metaphysical dilemmas existentialism sets out for us about the nature of being and the point of existence; but these cannot be disengaged from the political situation playing out around him, which intensifies the nausea he is struggling to keep at bay. One of the diary entries reads, 'Nothing. Existed', which is how any of us might feel after struggling to come to terms with our own disordered world.[14]

Roquentin has several bouts of nausea over the course of the novel, being repeatedly caught unaware by an episode, almost reflecting the chronic instability of European politics in the 1930s, when nothing could be taken for granted any more and socio-political breakdown seemed just round the corner as crisis followed crisis. His diary entries are from 1932, when social and political unrest, as in the street fighting going on between Nazis and Communists in Berlin (cited by Roquentin at one point), was rife throughout the continent. By 1938, when *Nausea* was published, the situation was even more grave as the Nazis had taken over in Germany and were asserting themselves menacingly against their neighbours, meaning that no-one could have been unaware of how bleak the immediate future was looking. Metaphysical and political absurdity seem interconnected at such points, leaving individuals at the mercy of the unexpected, which can disrupt their life at any point with little or no warning. There are many parallels to note between that period and our own in the last two decades or so, becoming more marked year by year. Indeed, it could be argued that we are now going through our own version of existentialist times, marked by a similar sense of precipitous decline in political, moral, and economic terms (even in health terms as well, as the Covid pandemic brought home to us so forcefully; yet another encounter with the absurd that humanity was badly caught out by and remains vulnerable to as the virus goes on mutating). Authoritarian- and totalitarian-minded regimes, for example, are increasingly evident on the international stage; Vladimir Putin's Russia providing a model for the many unscrupulous others keen to go down that route—*Autocracy, Inc.* as Anne Applebaum's book collectively dubs them.[15] No nation can consider itself entirely safe from such a fate, meaning that more bad, and probably very bad things undoubtedly lie waiting ahead for all of us.

Going back to the work of Sartre, this study will reassess existentialist philosophy in terms of contemporary socio-political events and concerns and its implications for us now. The contention will be that existentialist thought provides a particularly appropriate framework for processing said events and concerns and establishing what our priorities ought to be. It is a philosophy that comes into its own in times of socio-political disorder, when the Absurd looms ever larger in our daily experience. For many of us there is no other way to define Brexit, the Trump presidency, the Russian invasion of Ukraine, and the war in Gaza than as instances of the Absurd. The same can be said of the hold that conspiracy theory seems to be exerting on the popular imagination, or the continued reliance on fossil fuels despite the extreme weather events that their use is generating on an ever more frequent, and manifestly disastrous, basis. It is worth noting that the EU's Copernicus Climate Change Service has declared that 2024 was the hottest year on record. The problem being that those responsible for such phenomena do not recognise the absurdity of what they are doing, regarding their actions as justified instead by their own particular belief system—that being a particularly aggressive form of neoliberal capitalism where profit dominates all other considerations, including, dangerously for the rest of us, the environment. The end result is exploitation on a grand scale with no thought of the consequences—and these look set to be dire.

Tech billionaires may blithely hold forth about terraforming planets such as Mars for humanity to colonise (Elon Musk has been pictured wearing a tee-shirt proclaiming 'Occupy Mars' and has plans to build a city there), but as a solution for replacing Earth as our home in the near future because we have made it unliveable, that has to remain in the realms of fantasy. This is a point that Kelly and Zach Weinersmith emphasise in their book, *A City on Mars*, the subtitle of which very pointedly asks us 'Have We Really Thought This Through?'. The answer is no, we have not. As they go on to argue in a follow-up article: 'To be clear, we don't think humanity will be saved by leaving Earth. Solving our problems here, now, is more important than a short-term rush elsewhere'.[16] The fantasy of the short-term rush may well keep the tech billionaire class and their followers buzzing, but meanwhile, as far as the rest of us are concerned, climate crisis intensifies rapidly, with little of real substance being done to stop it. Mars can never be anything more than a distraction from dealing with that situation and we delude ourselves to think otherwise.

It could, sadly enough, be said that we find ourselves in a period when *Nausea* resonates all too vividly in our everyday experience; where 'That filthy thing' has come to seem an entirely accurate description of our current plight in a world increasingly under the control of authoritarians, unscrupulous corporate entities and climate sceptics, all reinforcing each other's power. To find ourselves again in existentialist times presents us with an intriguing possibility: what if we were to deploy Sartre's *Nausea*, and the existentialist philosophy layered into it, to put the causes of that plight into perspective (I am tempted to say into a far more realistic perspective)? That is the aim of the study that follows.

Themes and Structure

The central chapters in the book will deal with the problems set for our times by political authoritarianism, climate crisis and universal theories claiming to be the only valid explanation for the state of our world. Collectively these demonstrate how depressingly widespread bad faith, one of Sartre's central concerns, has become and how desperate the need is for authentic behaviour to challenge its unmistakably negative impact on our lifestyle. Chapter 2 therefore will go into more detail about the socio-political background that prompted a response of nausea from authors such as Sartre in the late 1930s, to draw out the parallels (and they are many) with our current state. There are worrying correspondences to note in the rise of political authoritarianism in the West and the clear threat it poses to democratic principles there (more under threat than they have been since the days of the Cold War). Rogue politicians and rogue states are asserting themselves ever more forcefully, and shamelessly, and Donald Trump winning the presidency for the second time can only encourage them further. I have been writing this work over the course of the American election campaign and the portents of what will happen once Trump takes office are not good. He is openly authoritarian with dictatorial leanings (even his ex-government aides have labelled him a fascist), so we face the alarming prospect of America too joining a desperate club that can name Hungary, Belarus and Italy in Europe as members, as well as India, China and North Korea in the East. This is by no means an exhaustive list either, with South American nations such as Argentina and Venezuela beginning to act in a similar manner. Dictatorships can spread like a virus, as they clearly did in the pre-war period—first Mussolini, then Hitler, then Franco, almost in a series of tribute acts. Nausea then only too readily translates into nausea now when we survey the landscape of recent politics, which, as in the 1930s, is becoming increasingly hostile to democratic ideals, and indeed to the whole notion of political opposition.[17] Dissent of any kind is being suppressed in a systematic fashion by the new autocratic order, yet another campaign that can spread like a virus and create new tribute acts.

Democracy is not a perfect system by any means, and there is little doubt that it is badly in need of updating (the 'first past the post' electoral system, as in place in the UK and elsewhere, being a leading candidate for this, as various defenders of proportional representation keep arguing[18]), but authoritarian rule benefits no-one except those in power. And those in power have a well-documented tendency to want to extend that power over the rest of us indefinitely. Even a flawed form of democracy is preferable to that fate; democracy is open to alteration from within, whereas autocracy is set up to prevent any attempt at that. Despite my reservations, and socialist orientation politically, I will be arguing the case for both democracy and liberalism throughout this book, identifying with their anti-authoritarianism above all else. They can be taken as shorthand, therefore, for 'anti-far right' and 'anti-autocracy'. There is a huge ideological divide involved here and it is far more important to know which side one would rather be on, and prepared to defend, than to quibble over the differences of opinion on that side (as those on the left in particular have had an unfortunate tendency to do down the years, making it easy for the far right to mock their apparent disarray). Pragmatism is crucial in such instances and I will do my best to adhere to that.

All defenders of democracy would do well, however, to heed Laura Spinney's claim that '[t]oday, most of us who think we are living in democracies are in fact living in systems closer to oligarchies, where the governing is done by small, usually wealthy elites'.[19] Part of the problem here is what has been dubbed 'elective dictatorship', where a governing party has the power to do whatever it wants if it has a large enough parliamentary majority: a situation which is about to be tested as to its limits in the new American administration from 2025 onwards, one has to suspect. If a party wins several elections in a row, as can sometimes happen, the sense of entitlement it creates amongst the ruling party can make the 'dictatorship' aspect even more pronounced, which can soon erode faith in the democratic process. We need to set about 'reimagining', and reconstructing democracy, therefore—but not from a far-right perspective, which would be to reimagine and reconstruct it out of existence.

The threat of nausea now is further magnified by the phenomenon of climate crisis and the dread spectre of the irreversible tipping points it may bring, which forms the subject of Chap. 3. Those tipping points are looming alarmingly large: the Arctic in particular giving out unmistakable warning signs on that score, with temperatures substantially above modern records (and increasing rapidly each year). Ice sheets are breaking up regularly in both polar regions, holding out the prospect of frightening rises in sea levels, which could render large parts of the globe, such as the heavily populated coastal areas where so many major cities are located (London and New York for a start), uninhabitable. (The huge Thwaites Glacier on the West Antarctic ice sheet, roughly the size of the UK, is retreating at a rate that is causing great concern amongst climate scientists, for whom it could spell a 'doomsday' event.[20]) Climate crisis has been referred to as climate boiling by some environmentalists, to indicate how dire the situation is in danger of becoming for humanity. Yet fossil fuel continues to be the main method of generating power throughout the world, and the fossil-fuel industry is providing a master-class in bad faith in its refusal to acknowledge the scale of the problem. Or even that there is a problem at all in many cases, with climate change scepticism all too common a reaction amongst its management class, whose attention is firmly fixed on market performance and profit margins to the exclusion of all else (their shareholders likewise). Some other commentators have seen a role for existentialism in this debate, as in debates around town planning to cut down carbon emissions from traffic, for example (another issue which generates its own brand of sceptics, although not ones I would identify with as a philosophical sceptic), and these will be assessed also.[21]

Chapter 4 examines how belief in universal theories continues to have a detrimental impact on the public realm, treating conspiracy theories as a contemporary manifestation of this condition at its most sinister. Given that they can be generated by anything or everything, such theories form an all but perpetual backdrop to public life that we cannot escape from. (Some recent research suggests that using AI Chatbots can help reduce belief in these, although one does wonder how widely that could ever be implemented; or how willing believers would be to engage in the exercise either.[22] Conspiracists are rarely open to challenges to their position.) Universal theories, Marxism providing an outstanding example, claim that they are the only possible true explanation of phenomena and reject all competing theories, depending upon the uncritical belief of followers to maintain their authority and hold on public opinion; yet again, political opposition is put at risk as a concept. Bad faith is much in evidence here and arguments for authenticity particularly needed to counter it. The critical feature of authenticity, or good faith, is that it has to be chosen: it 'supposes a self-recovery of being which was previously corrupted. This self-recovery we shall call authenticity'.[23] In other words, it involves a deliberate move away from uncritical belief (interestingly enough, Sartre points out that there can be 'awakenings ... to good faith', which suggests that 'wokeness' might be an appropriate place to start from in spreading the message on authenticity[24]).

Existentialism is opposed to universal theories in general. Sartre, as David Caute summed it up, 'rejected all determinisms, whether Marxian, Freudian or behaviourist', although that created difficulties for him in a period when left-wing politics was strongly influenced by Marxism and the Communist Party was a very powerful force in France.[25] The trend in philosophy since existentialism has been very much anti-universal theory, as in the case of poststructuralism and postmodernism, so Sartre could be seen as a fellow-traveller there too (even if those movements have generally distanced themselves from him, if not always all that convincingly however[26]). That trend is less interested in finding an all-purpose theory itself than in analysing the, often very questionable, assumptions of the last generation or so of universal theories. Yet in public life universal theories still hold considerable power and influence—as they do in monotheistic religions, for example, often acting against what I would take to be the public interest. The late 1930s seem closer to our experience than is comfortable.

In the current socio-political situation, where climate change denialists, anti-woke protestors, and conspiracy theorists continue to poison public debate, a despair-induced nausea is a natural reaction from anyone of a liberal-minded outlook faced with such a toxic combination in the public sphere. The book's concluding chapter will therefore adopt, albeit reluctantly, a pessimistic line on where this is all leading and what it says about human psychology. It is a situation we are going to have to live with for the foreseeable future, given the way it has so ruthlessly colonised the online social media sector, keeping such far-fetched ideas in the public eye even if there is no evidence to back up their claims. Indeed, evidence to the contrary is simply ignored by the uncritical believer, for whom their theory is sacrosanct and does not have to be proved; either you sign up for it or you are not worth talking to and can be ignored. Nevertheless, we have to go on challenging this persistent drift into irrationality, developing a rigorous philosophical scepticism to counter it with as publicly, and widely, as we can. To be pessimistic is not the same thing, however, as giving up and thereby ceding victory to denialists and authoritarians in general. Existentialist times are never less than emotionally taxing and there are no easy solutions to the problems they generate, but they must not be allowed to defeat us: even if some high-profile thinkers, such as the philosopher John Gray have more or less given up, blaming all of our ills on liberals and their apparently misguided beliefs.[27] (Anti-wokeness is well on its way to becoming a universal theory in its own right it would seem, unwilling to accept criticism or to give any credence to alternative worldviews.) Yet another example of reading the present through the work of a prominent philosopher, this time Thomas Hobbes (at best a problematic choice in my view), Gray's is a doom-laden pessimism that predicts we are heading for 'global anarchy' and will just have to learn to live with this fate. Authoritarians would no doubt be only too happy if we did, allowing them to go on exploiting it to their advantage.

I will be returning to Gray's ideas on this topic later in the book, but I have claimed before that there is such a thing as a positive pessimism and that is what will be argued for here—a pessimism based on a cold-eyed realism rather than on despair.[28] Worst-case scenarios are scary to contemplate, but they can happen and there is no point in pretending otherwise. Interestingly enough, a *New Scientist* editorial recently suggested the value of such an attitude towards climate change, arguing that 'when it comes to climate modelling, some negative thinking could be a good thing. ... Instead of squeezing climate models until the numbers just about fit the 1.5 °C target, perhaps a more pessimistic outlook would better accelerate efforts to limit the damage'.[29] It strikes me that existentialism provides a particularly relevant basis for such an exercise in positive pessimism, and that Sartre's fellow-travelling credentials deserve to be advertised as much as possible to help facilitate this. I would certainly want to argue that we will find Sartre a far more useful fellow-traveller than Hobbes would ever be. Hobbes speaks to the right (particularly the far right), Sartre to the left, and I will take it from there.

Existentialism and the Freedom Dilemma

Existentialism prizes freedom above all else, although as with the philosophy itself it is a difficult concept to pin down with precision: 'freedom from' and 'freedom to' do not always align with each other, for example, very often clash in fact. Freedom to spread lies in the name of exercising the right to free speech gives an indication of the tangles one can get into on the subject—and one that the far right is proving only too willing to exploit. It is an open question as well whether libertarianism or neoliberal economics is really in the wider public interest, or whether in actuality they significantly reduce the freedom of large parts of the population of the democracies where they are entrenched. Freedom to do what you want is, it has to be noted, highly dependent on freedom from poverty (not to mention well-funded public services, which the far right inevitably want to cut, in line with their commitment to the 'small state' ethos). In a period like the 1930s, however, it was more obvious when one's most basic freedoms were under attack, with fascist regimes banning political opposition of any kind and clamping down ruthlessly on freedom of expression—to the extent of imprisoning, or even murdering, those who disobeyed (communism had the same sorry record under Stalin). Such things are happening in totalitarian states around the world at present, and curbing freedom of expression is becoming a factor even in democratic polities; one has to wonder how much of a battleground the latter will turn out to be as the second Trump presidency unfolds.

Most of us are observing the change in the political climate from the sidelines with a horrified fascination, as well as a debilitating sense of our powerlessness to prevent it from becoming ever more pronounced. Roquentin's plight is ours in that regard, with a fear that we too are doing no more than just 'existing' on the fringes and that our activities are probably meaningless in the wider scheme of things. Anyone who has ever pursued an extended research project such as a doctoral thesis or academic book will be familiar with that feeling, as we follow our own version of the history of the Marquis de Rollebon's life that Roquentin is working on with seemingly decreasing interest. We too have to find our way out of that condition, even if it shapes up into a series of taxing struggles full of tough, often ambiguous, choices that can induce episodes of pessimism; that is the dilemma that freedom poses us and a new age of nausea forces us to address as bravely as possible. The existentialist line would have to be that we have no choice but to engage with the world in that way, that to do otherwise would be wilfully unauthentic, and I will be fully in agreement with that. Fellow-travelling with Sartre will start from that premise.

Existentialism and the Right

At this point, it is worth saying a few words about the ideological orientation of this study. I have already made several references to the far right, mostly uncomplimentary (and unapologetically so, I hasten to add), and there will be many more to come, which no doubt makes my own political position fairly obvious. As I indicated earlier, I am on the left, but I concede that not all right-wing thinkers are as anti-democratic and authoritarian as those on the far right. If you want to back democracy, as I will be doing repeatedly throughout this work (despite its many flaws and need for constant improvement to uphold its ideals), then you have to accept that there is a right and left end to the political spectrum and to be willing to engage with those on the opposite side from yourself. I can understand conservatism in politics, although I do not agree with the bulk of its assumptions, but I am not suggesting that it has no place in democracy or should be dismissed out of hand; it has too firm a basis in Western culture to claim that. Existentialism can be used to defend democracy, but not, I will be arguing, the political programme of the far right. It is the latter that I will be attacking, therefore, not right-wing politics in general. The traditional right accepts the fact of opposition, whereas the far right does not: yet another critical dividing line to be borne in mind. What the far right encourages, and directs its appeal towards, is bigotry and prejudice, which have no place in a democratic system; when that becomes a political tactic then we have passed beyond democracy, as existentialists would be quick to point out.

As to the approach to existentialism that I will be adopting overall, my intention is to be flexible in how I use Sartre's main concepts, trying to widen their range as much as I can in order to open up new debates and challenge existing perspectives. The density of Sartre's writing notwithstanding, existentialism did after all turn out to be a philosophy with a significant popular appeal. As Sarah Bakewell notes, in France as the war ended: 'Every fashionable person wanted to learn about it, every Establishment institution fretted about it, and almost every journalist seemed to be using it to make a living'.[30] Those concepts still resonate over time as well, inviting constant reinterpretation and adaptation in terms of cultural change and how to go about analysing it. What they suggest, and how and why they resonate, will be more important to my argument, therefore, than any precision as to their meaning (it has to be noted that authenticity is left a fairly open concept by Sartre anyway, not really being developed much further than as the opposite of bad faith). Ally speaks of the need 'to stretch and bend his thought here and there, without breaking it', when using Sartre as a basis for addressing ecological issues.[31] I will be adopting a similar approach across a range of concerns in the contemporary world to see what it can reveal about these: that is what it means to be a fellow-traveller. That will particularly be the case when it comes to bad faith, authenticity, and the absurd, which have a whole new range of situations they can be applied to now—and will be over the course of the book, in order to emphasise just how much of a fellow-traveller Sartre can, and should be for us. Nausea, too, invites similar treatment in the way it illustrates the complex interaction of the emotional, the philosophical and the political that is the individual's lot in societies in trouble. It constitutes a powerful metaphor for that condition. Yes, things are bad, heading towards very bad: now, how can we survive that? Let us explore how existentialism can help us in answering that question.

Notes

1. Jean-Paul Sartre, *Nausea* (1938), trans. Robert Baldick, Harmondsworth: Penguin, 1965, p. 32.
2. *The Guardian*, Journal section, 10 July 2023, p. 2.

3. See, for example, Stuart Sim, *Post-Truth, Scepticism and Power*, London: Palgrave Macmillan, 2019, and Stuart Sim, *Daniel Defoe's A Journal of the Plague Year and Covid-19: A Tale of Two Pandemics*, London: Palgrave Macmillan, 2023.
4. Sarah Bakewell, *At the Existentialist Café: Freedom, Being, and Apricot Cocktails*, London: Vintage, 2017, p. 34.
5. Jean-Paul Sartre, *Existentialism and Humanism* (1946), trans. Philip Mairet, London: Methuen, 1973, p. 28.
6. Ibid.
7. Jean-Paul Sartre, *The Age of Reason* (1945), trans. Eric Sutton, London: Penguin, 1986; *The Reprieve* (1945), trans. Eric Sutton, London: Penguin, 1986; and *Iron in the Soul* (1949), trans. Gerard Hopkins, London: Penguin, 2002.
8. Jean-Paul Sartre, *Being and Nothingness: An Essay on Phenomenological Ontology* (1943), trans. Hazel E. Barnes, London: Methuen, 1969.
9. Robert Jenrick, 'Many of Britain's Former Colonies Owe Us a Debt of Gratitude for the Inheritance We Left Them', *Mail Online*, 28 October 2024 (accessed 10 November 2024).
10. Matthew C. Ally, *Ecology and Existence: Bringing Sartre to the Water's Edge*, Lanham, MD and London: Lexington Books, 2017, and Matthew C. Ally and Damon Boria, eds, *Earthly Engagements: Reading Sartre After the Holocaust*, Lanham, MD and London: Lexington Books, 2023.
11. Ronald Aronson, 'Why Sartre, Today?', in Ally, *Earthly Engagements*, pp. ix–xiv (p. ix).
12. Ibid., p. xi.
13. William L. McBride, 'Sartre and Problems in the Philosophy of Ecology – with a Thirty-Year Update', ibid., pp. 13–26.
14. Sartre, *Nausea*, p. 149.
15. Anne Applebaum, *Autocracy, Inc.: The Dictators Who Want to Run the World*, New York and London: Allen Lane, 2024.
16. Kelly and Zach Weinersmith, *A City on Mars: Can We Settle Space, Should We Settle Space, and Have We Really Thought This Through?*, London: Penguin, 2023, and 'Life on Mars', *New Scientist*, 16 November 2024, pp. 48–51 (p. 51).
17. I cover this topic in more detail in Stuart Sim, *A Call to Dissent: Defending Democracy Against Extremism and Populism*, Edinburgh: Edinburgh University Press, 2022.
18. See, for example, Vernon Bogdanor, *What is Proportional Representation?: A Guide to the Issues*, Oxford: Martin Robertson, 1984.
19. Laura Spinney, 'Reimagining Democracy', *New Scientist*, 5 October 2024, pp. 32–5 (p. 32).
20. Alison George, '"Doomsday" Glacier is Headed for Calamitous Collapse', *New Scientist*, 28 September 2024, p. 13.

21. See, for example, Markus Moos, 'Existentialism: A Guiding Philosophy for Tackling Climate Change in Cities?', *The Conversation*, https://theconversation.com/existentialism-a-guiding-philosophy-for-tackling-climate-change-in-cities (accessed 1 December, 2023), and Paul Gyllenhammer, 'Sartre and Heidegger on Social Deformation and the *Anthropocene*', *Sartre Studies International*, 24:2 (2018), pp. 25–44.
22. Chris Stokel-Walker, 'Chatbots Can Persuade Conspiracy Theorists to Change Their Minds', *New Scientist*, 20 April 2024, p. 17.
23. Sartre, *Being and Nothingness*, p. 70 (note 9).
24. Ibid., p. 50.
25. David Caute, Introduction to Sartre, *The Age of Reason*, pp. v–xviii (p. viii).
26. For an argument establishing connections between the thought of Sartre and those later movements, see Nik Farrell Fox, *The New Sartre: Explorations in Postmodernism*, London and New York: Continuum, 2003.
27. John Gray, *The New Leviathans: Thoughts After Liberalism*, London: Allen Lane, 2023.
28. Stuart Sim, *A Philosophy of Pessimism*, London: Reaktion Books; Chicago: University of Chicago Press, 2015.
29. 'Climate Pessimism', *New Scientist*, 20 April 2024, p. 5.
30. Sarah Bakewell, *At the Existentialist Café*, p. 165.
31. Ally, *Ecology and Existence*, p. 5.

References

Ally, Matthew C., *Ecology and Existence: Bringing Sartre to the Water's Edge*, Lanham, MD and London: Lexington Books, 2017.
———. and Damon Boria, eds, *Earthly Engagements: Reading Sartre After the Holocene*, Lanham, MD and London: Lexington Books, 2023.
Applebaum, Anne, *Autocracy, Inc.: The Dictators Who Want to Run the World*, New York and London: Allen Lane, 2024.
Aronson, Ronald, 'Why Sartre, Today?', in Matthew C. Ally and Damon Boria, eds, *Earthly Engagements: Reading Sartre After the Holocene*, Lanham, MD and London: Lexington Books, 2023, pp. ix–xiv.
Bakewell, Sarah, *At the Existentialist Café: Freedom, Being, and Apricot Cocktails*, London: Vintage, 2017.
Bogdanor, Vernon, *What is Proportional Representation?: A Guide to the Issues*, Oxford: Martin Robertson, 1984.
'Climate Pessimism', *New Scientist*, 20 April 2024, p. 5.
Fox, Nik Farrell, *The New Sartre: Explorations in Postmodernism*, London and New York: Continuum, 2003.
George, Alison, '"Doomsday" Glacier is Headed for Calamitous Collapse', *New Scientist*, 28 September 2024, p. 13.

Gray, John, *The New Leviathans: Thoughts After Liberalism*, London: Allen Lane, 2023.
The Guardian, Journal section, 10 July 2023, p. 2.
Gyllenhammer, Paul, 'Sartre and Heidegger on Social Deformation and the Anthropocene', *Sartre Studies International*, 24:2 (2018), pp. 25–44.
Jenrick, Robert, 'Many of Britain's Former Colonies Owe Us a Debt of Gratitude for the Inheritance We Left Them', *Mail Online*, 28 October 2024 (accessed 10 November, 2024).
McBride, William L., 'Sartre and Problems in the Philosophy of Ecology – with a Thirty-Year Update', in Matthew C. Ally and Damon Boria, eds, *Earthly Engagements: Reading Sartre After the Holocene*, Lanham, MD and London: Lexington Books, 2023, pp. 13–26.
Moos, Markus, 'Existentialism: A Guiding Philosophy for Tackling Climate Change in Cities?', *The Conversation*, https://theconversation.com/existentialism-a-guiding-philosophy-for-tackling-climate-change-in-cities (accessed 1 December, 2023).
Sartre, Jean-Paul, *Nausea* (1938), trans. Robert Baldick, Harmondsworth: Penguin, 1965.
———. *Being and Nothingness: An Essay on Phenomenological Ontology* (1943), trans. Hazel E. Barnes, London: Methuen, 1969.
———. *The Age of Reason* (1945), trans. Eric Sutton, London: Penguin, 2001.
———. *The Reprieve* (1945), trans. Eric Sutton, London: Penguin, 1986.
———. *Existentialism and Humanism* (1946), trans. Philip Mairet, London: Methuen, 1973.
———. *Iron in the Soul* (1949), trans. Gerard Hopkins, London: Penguin, 2002.
Sim, Stuart, *A Philosophy of Pessimism*, London: Reaktion Books; Chicago: University of Chicago Press, 2015.
———. *Post-Truth, Scepticism and Power*, London: Palgrave Macmillan, 2019.
———. *A Call to Dissent: Defending Democracy Against Extremism and Populism*, Edinburgh: Edinburgh University Press, 2022.
———. *Daniel Defoe's* A Journal of the Plague Year *and Covid-19: A Tale of Two Pandemics*, London: Palgrave Macmillan, 2023.
Spinney, Laura, 'Reimagining Democracy', *New Scientist*, 5 October 2024, pp. 32–5.
Stokel-Walker, Chris, 'Chatbots Can Persuade Conspiracy Theorists to Change Their Minds', *New Scientist*, 20 April, 2024, p. 17.
Weinersmith, Kelly and Zach, *A City on Mars: Can We Settle Space, Should We Settle Space, and Have We Really Thought This Through?*, London: Penguin, 2023.
———. 'Life on Mars', *New Scientist*, 16 November 2024, pp. 48–51.

CHAPTER 2

Political Authoritarianism

Abstract The socio-political background to the publication of Jean-Paul Sartre's *Nausea* in the late 1930s, and the extent to which this prefigures the rise of authoritarianism in our own day, is discussed in this chapter. The lack of authenticity in contemporary political life is explored (and deplored), as well as the worrying increase in the influence of the far right on democratic processes internationally. It is argued that this is a trend which has to be challenged wherever it can be by supporters of democracy. Sartre's concept of bad faith, and its application to current ideological conflicts, is analysed in detail, particularly the way it has become standard practice in many Western democracies as well as in the world's various autocracies. The implications of world powers like America becoming progressively more right wing in their policies is also discussed, and the need for this to be carefully monitored is emphasised.

Keywords Authoritarianism • Jean-Paul Sartre • Democracy • *Nausea* • Autocracy • Authenticity • Denialism • Bad faith • Donald Trump • Fascism

In this chapter I will be considering the socio-political background that could prompt a response of nausea in the late 1930s, to try and work out whether we are in a comparable state now that should make us rethink how we are conducting our politics. Right away there are some worrying correspondences to report in terms of a rise of political authoritarianism in the West and the very substantial danger that presents to democratic principles there. For a long time now authoritarianism has been thought to be a primarily non-Western phenomenon, more common in Africa, Asia and South America than in Western Europe or North America. Yet here we are observing it spreading into our own sphere and forcing us to rethink our political objectives and how they can be defended from both internal and external enemies (while being aware that the far right interpret these entities in an entirely different way than democrats do; to them, democracy is the enemy). As noted earlier, rogue politicians and rogue states are increasingly in evidence all around the world scene, often collaborating with each other in their deliberately disruptive political schemes, as Anne Applebaum documents. The more they combine their forces the more we have to fear, because democracy can be a fragile entity, very vulnerable to being corrupted from within by disinformation campaigns of the kind that authoritarians are so adept at deploying. Propaganda has a long and ethically dubious history, but the industry that has grown up around disinformation has taken it onto a new level in terms of cultural impact (the Russian state under Vladimir Putin has gone into this in a big way, signalling their highly dubious ideological intentions). Its role in affecting various national elections, the USA being a particular target and the Republican Party the main beneficiary, is only just coming to be understood, although how to stop that from happening is not all that clear: democracies are particularly at risk on that score, their open and accessible nature making them relatively easy to infiltrate. All of us are now regularly exposed to this material whether we want to be or not, it has simply become part of everyday discourse, something that cannot be avoided if we are internet users.

The war in Ukraine has also had the disturbing effect of revealing the weakness of the Western democratic order in general, given that Russian aggression in the area has been allowed to continue over a period of years now, from Russia's controversial annexation of the Crimea in 2014 onwards. For all its moral support, the West has been notably careful to avoid direct confrontation with Russia (fear of its nuclear arsenal promoting caution). Whether Ukraine can be restored to its pre-war boundaries is becoming increasingly problematic therefore, with longer-term geopolitical implications it would be hard to predict; future generations can harbour resentment for a very long time and it can break out in unexpected ways. Parallels with the fate of Czechoslovakia are all too obvious, with the same accusations of appeasement being made about some of the plans put forward as to how to bring the conflict to an end. Such as that Ukraine cedes a significant part of its territory to Russia, for example, as the Czechs were recommended to do to Nazi Germany by the British and French governments in their desperate, although ultimately fruitless, attempts to avoid war. Autocratic governments such as Putin's are not likely to back down without some tangible gains after waging a war for this long; to do anything less would be in their view to lose face.

The degree of self-deception involved in such crises illustrates how easily bad faith can undermine entire social systems, making it clear how critical it is to develop an authentic response to the harm this is causing, particularly its generation of a politics based largely on appeals to prejudice and bigotry. That there is such a sizeable audience for this is a sign that democracy is not working as well as it should be; at such points significant fault-lines reveal themselves in the system, given that it is designed to prioritise reason over emotion. At its worst this style of politics can inspire threats and even physical violence from the general public against candidates for office (as the USA experienced throughout the 2024 presidential election campaign), a trend that is becoming more widespread throughout the democratic system in general. In fact, violence and death threats have turned into standard elements there, with few politicians failing to be exposed to these at some point in their career, which is hardly a selling point for prospective candidates for office: many will just decide it is not worth going through such trouble and decline to put themselves forward (or stand down earlier than they had planned). A disturbing air of crudity has crept into Western political life of late, and it can seem as if this exercise in bad faith is being rewarded, which is not a good feeling for the democratically minded. That things really are very bad there cannot be denied, and they do bring the 1930s to mind as if we had not learned the lessons we should have from the dreadful war this precipitated.

Existentialism can be brought to bear against this turn to prejudice and anti-wokeness, and it can be a very positive philosophy in that respect; as indicated before, it is temperamentally opposed to bigotry in any form. But that positive side always has to contend with its dark side of absurdity—depressingly regularly demonstrated when war and violent conflict are resorted to by political authoritarians, as they are almost by reflex (Ukraine being only one amongst many such events in recent history; Sudan offering another, where civil war between rival army factions is creating havoc amongst its population, as is also the case in Haiti). The sense of nausea that keeps overwhelming Sartre's protagonist Roquentin seems just as applicable to our contemporary condition, where we are beset not just by political problems such as the ones mentioned, but by the spectre of climate change and the irreversible tipping points it may bring (indeed, increasingly is bringing). Put all those phenomena together and we can be said to have entered a 'new age of nausea', the very lowest point of existentialist times, where the world no longer seems to be making any sense and absurdity to have taken over. All the more so when the volatile situation in the Middle East is factored in, as it no doubt will have to be into the indefinite future, constituting a differend, in Jean-François Lyotard's terminology, of a particularly intractable kind (a differend being a fundamentally irresolvable dispute, where each side is in effect speaking a different language, which excludes the assumptions and claims of the other[1]).

Political differends do seem to be proliferating at a rapid rate as well, and that is a state of affairs the far right will always thrive in; discord is what they invariably seek to further their interests. At the individual level this can all be deeply distressing, and that is the level at which Roquentin is suffering. There is nothing quite like a large-scale socio-political crisis, driven by utterly ruthless players—demagogues, dictators, autocrats, et al.—who are prepared to go to drastic lengths to exert their domination over others, to make us aware of just how insignificant we are as individuals, how little power we have to wield on our own behalf. That is when we are most at risk of succumbing to nausea, so Roquentin is another of our fellow-travellers, someone whose extreme reaction to unforeseen events is entirely understandable and easy to identify with.

Nausea's Background

By the late 1930s totalitarianism was turning into all but the norm in European politics, led by fascist regimes in Germany, Italy and Spain, and communism in Russia. The 'strong leader' principle was much in evidence at the time, severely distorting the political process by passing laws banning opposition to those in power, Hitler and Mussolini setting the standard in that regard. That is a trend which has become noticeable again of late, even in ostensibly liberal democracies. No-one particularly likes opposition when they are in power, which is precisely why it is so necessary, in the hope of keeping those wielding it as honest as possible. Strong leaders, however, just do not admit the viability of viewpoints other than their own, their natural reaction being to suppress these by whatever means they consider necessary ('terminating with extreme prejudice' being amongst these as anti-fascist campaigners can find out the hard way). Politics is an extended exercise in bullying for strong leaders, who make their lack of respect for others very plain (as both Hitler and Mussolini consistently and blatantly did), forcing their opponents into desperate moves to try and keep some kind of dialogue going. Appeasement became one of the tactics adopted against the fascist powers in the hope this would placate their increasingly aggressive dictators, with Czechoslovakia the unfortunate victim, although this did not rein them in to any significant degree nor halt the slide towards war. Appeasement was viewed as weakness by fascists and greater and ever more unreasonable demands made as a result. This is an all too predictable outcome which always needs to be borne in mind when dealing with such movements: they operate according to a different playbook, one notably lacking in moral constraints. You fellow-travel with fascists at your peril, as a generation of European political figures were to find to their cost.

Seen against this backdrop the despairing tone of a work like *Nausea* is not hard to understand. Roquentin's growing sense of the pointlessness of his intellectual endeavours as a historian is emblematic of the plight of the ordinary individual confronted by such a bewildering, and seemingly out of control, political situation. Differends on such a scale as this can be desperately demoralising, as we know from our own recent experiences of Ukraine and Gaza, which offer no obvious diplomatic solutions that are likely to hold over time: indeed, diplomacy finds itself confronted by the equivalent of a black hole at such points. The more unfortunate side of such situations is that they are soon overtaken by others, of at least equal and sometimes even greater seriousness, meaning that they can fester away indefinitely in the background as attention shifts elsewhere. They will always have the opportunity to do that too, as new differends will just keep on emerging in the interim, deflecting public interest as they come to light—what next after Ukraine and Gaza? (already the conflict in the latter has spread to Lebanon, Iran and Syria). Eventually they can take on an air of insuperability as they persist over the years, which only serves to deepen the sense of grievance of all the parties involved, making rapprochement less and less likely to occur. Authoritarian regimes are expert at exploiting such long-running disputes when it suits them to do so, working up prejudice amongst the public to further their own ideological ends—disinformation coming into its own in such cases. At which point appeasement very often works its way back on to the agenda, to as little beneficial effect as usual: bullies are never impressed by it, since it only succeeds in showing the desperation of their opponents.

The *Roads to Freedom* trilogy maps out how political authoritarianism can quickly come to dominate the political scene and control its agenda. It covers the traumatic period from just before the infamous Munich conference between Hitler and the British and French governments in 1938, promising 'peace in our time', through to the fall of France in the early stages of World War II after the devastating German invasion. Its characters find their lives completely disrupted by the sudden turn of events, forced to work out how to respond to them with little to fall back on for support. The abrupt shifts from one character's thoughts to another's that Sartre keeps making throughout the narrative captures the sense of confusion of the situation. There is a foreboding quality to the atmosphere they are all living in, until the point when their worst fears become reality and they face a future dictated by totalitarianism of a particularly vicious and unforgiving kind, committed to destroying any who stand in the way of its drive to ideological domination. The vulnerability of the individual comes through very strongly over the interlocking narratives with their air of impending doom, providing a stark reminder of the need to live authentically as well as the sheer difficulty of doing so in particularly trying circumstances. War, occupation by enemy forces, prison camps, and forced labour (the fate of the train carrying captured French soldiers over the course of the final book of the trilogy, *Iron in the Soul*), collectively constitute a depressing backdrop to daily life that even the most optimistic will struggle to overcome.[2] As one of the characters, the philosophy teacher Mathieu, muses in *The Reprieve*, thinking back about his experiences in the period since the last war: 'now the war is there, my life is dead: *that* was my life: everything must be started afresh'.[3] Afresh, but with no guarantee as to what events will bring or how to adapt to them.

We can certainly identify with the reaction of the characters in the trilogy, particularly when it comes to *The Reprieve*, as we scan the news each day to discover if the situation in Ukraine and the Middle East has deteriorated further. Each time we are hoping to find that the worst has been avoided and that diplomacy can come to our collective aid. In other words what we are looking for is evidence of a reprieve, while remaining aware that it may prove to be no more than that, and that things could suddenly, catastrophically, go wrong at any moment. Unsurprisingly, this is emotionally very draining, and a huge test of one's capacity for authenticity. Many will just draw into themselves in such circumstances, as Roquentin does every time he listens to the record of 'One of These Days' while sitting in his local cafe. But opting out of everyday life in that way, seductive though it can be as a means of respite, cannot resolve one's problems, or society's either, in the longer term.

Authoritarianism Now

Authoritarianism never really went away after the two world wars, but it did decline, at least in the West, which set itself up as a liberal democratic bloc in opposition to the still militantly authoritarian, communist-led, Eastern powers of Russia and China (plus their various satellites). Even the collapse of communism in Russia has not brought an end to authoritarianism there, however, with the Putin regime becoming progressively more dictatorial in style (Soviet light one might say, although not always all that light, as their invasion of Ukraine shows), with the same uncompromising attitude towards dissent. Elections in Russia now are no less a sham than they were in its Soviet days, with the outcome a foregone conclusion ('fake democracy' one might call it). As it is Putin who makes the rules, and Putin who enforces and monitors them, Putin always wins. The electorate has no meaningful role to play in the process and, without putting its personal safety at risk, no means of challenging the system; the few who do, soon find themselves up against the entire state machine and most likely imprisoned unless they leave the country.

As for China, it may be a more open country economically than it was in the earlier days of communist rule, but politically the Party is in as much control as ever. In the same manner as in Russia, elections are no more than ceremonial affairs because everyone knows who is going to win. All opposition is brutally put down if it is ever openly expressed, as it has been in Hong Kong on several occasions of late, for example. The promises made by the Party after the end of British rule in the colony in 1997, that a more democratic system would be maintained there than in mainland China, with protection in place for civil rights, have gradually been eroded and an authoritarian regime has been imposed on the population. International protests, particularly from the UK, have had no impact—as they rarely do with such regimes.

It is sad to see in this context that so many Western governments too have been making it increasingly difficult to hold public protests, for so long regarded as a defining characteristic of a democratic society, a right to be respected by governments of whatever political persuasion (I should emphasise that means peaceful protests, which can be a point of contention of course, depending on how 'peaceful' is interpreted by the relevant authorities). This has led to the police in the UK being given sweeping powers to prevent public marches protesting against government policies, and similar action has been taken in several other Western European nations in the wake of a definite rightward shift in political life there. Once again it is the paradox of democrats being all in favour of political opposition, until it is directed against them when in power, at which point they will do what they can to block it: another of democracy's fault-lines becoming apparent. Under the cover of 'public order', it is possible to push through manifestly anti-democratic restrictions on what can and cannot be said or done by the general public, a policy which a compliant right-wing press will almost invariably support, stirring up the social media network to no good effect in the process. Protestors against inaction over climate change are beginning to find themselves on the front line of this law and order initiative, leading to a certain amount of demonisation in the right-wing media, who treat them as yet another outbreak of the wokeness they are constantly warning us against. Law and order is a well-known staple of right-wing ideology of course, and yet another concept very open to interpretation: more and more frequently that interpretation is against the protestors, with harsh sentences being handed out to those arrested.

The encroachment of the right, particularly the extreme right, into liberal democracies is a very worrying trend, to be seen of late notably in France, Germany, Italy, the Netherlands and the UK. America is yet another troublesome issue, with the Republican Party there moving further and further away from the democratic ideals on which the country was founded in support of the totalitarian regime-sympathising Donald Trump, a great admirer of dictators in general. (That an American presidential candidate could ever campaign on the promise of becoming a dictator, and get away with it, would have been unthinkable before he came on the scene. It sets an alarming precedent in that regard.) Such movements may peter out, or at least reduce in influence, in the next few years and the worst-case scenario may not come to pass. Even so, we know that it did in the 1930s and 40s, and that nations can be subverted by such movements if they are determined enough (which can extend to being violent enough, which almost goes without saying when it comes to fascists, for whom this is all but second nature). It could happen just about anywhere and America at present looks particularly susceptible. Even if they do not always perform all that well in elections (democracies usually having set up various hurdles to try and forestall such an outcome), the extreme right cannot be underestimated. Elections can always be corrupted, or even bypassed altogether if extremists feel conditions are favourable enough for an attempt at a coup (with even America showing itself to be vulnerable to this response in the aftermath of the 2020 elections, when the Capitol was attacked by a mob of aggrieved Trump supporters in a bid to prevent the result being ratified). They have no conscience to hold them back from seizing power, whether in an already authoritarian system or a liberal democracy playing by the rules. Going by the rules is not an extremist characteristic, which leaves liberal democracies at a distinct disadvantage: more than something of a differend to be noted in play there, one would want to suggest.

Denialism has become all but an ideology for extremists everywhere, who can be relied on to deny whatever their opponents say, regardless of what evidence they can present for it, preferring this tactic to engaging in any meaningful debate. Even to acknowledge that there was any basis for debate would be considered as weakness by denialists. As we shall see as we work our way through the study's other issues, such as climate change and universal theories, denialism is proving a growing threat to the democratic ethos worldwide. Populism and denialism are all but turning into synonymous terms, further deepening the divides in our political life and the 'culture wars' they are so time consumingly, and utterly pointlessly, generating. The more the left and centre are drawn into such 'wars', the more the far right can dictate the agenda to their advantage by claiming that free speech is under attack: a situation that will always be difficult for democrats to negotiate their way out of with any great sense of confidence.

Anne Applebaum's *Autocracy, Inc.* reveals the scale of the problem that has built up in recent years, and it is sobering to reflect on it. Dictators, and would-be dictators, are all around us, with the common aim of putting an end to liberal democracy: a group, as Applebaum describes them, 'bound not by ideology but rather by a ruthless, single-minded determination to preserve their personal wealth and power' (I would want to define that as an ideology under the heading of 'totalitarianism' however).[4] Capitalism, as currently constituted anyway, does not exactly help matters either in this respect, given that those who lead giant corporations, the tech ones particularly, are all too prone to act as autocrats as well and have the financial power to do so. There is little doubt that the owners of the major social media platforms, figures such as Mark Zuckerberg and Elon Musk, have more effect on human behaviour and world politics than do many national governments. This is not at all a healthy situation for democracy as a system, as such figures are not accountable to the general public in the way their political counterparts are. Few of these cohorts could be described as advocates for democracy, their goals lie elsewhere (basically, in endlessly increasing their personal power and revenue streams). Musk, for example, has declared himself to be a free-speech absolutist, with the result that X has turned into a repository for hate speech, which no democracy wants or needs—but no democracy at present quite seems to know how to deal with when so brazenly marketed by such a powerful figure with such vast resources behind him. The dividing line between free speech and hate speech looks set to be an issue of heated debate between left and right for quite some time to come, which will no doubt benefit Musk's revenue streams. Hate speech can be profitable.

It is notable as well how many such corporate heads are drawn to creating monopolies for their product, buying up competitors to remove opposition so they can control their area of operation much in the way that political dictators do. Governments may try to regulate this tendency, monopolies officially being considered against the public interest in democracies, but there are limits as to what they can achieve when faced with the constant churn and general unpredictability of the business world and the financial markets. The autocratic impulse is more widespread than is perhaps being recognised. It is certainly well embedded in global capitalism, which means that it affects everyone's life in some way or other, globalisation has long since seen to that. Neither is it all that fussy about what regimes it deals with; moral considerations being a lesser concern for its large organisations, as is bad faith (my next topic below).

Politics and Unauthenticity

Few areas of human endeavour exhibit as many examples of bad faith as politics so consistently does. Unauthentic behaviour there is rife, even in democracies; in fact, the way that democratic systems have developed in the West positively encourages this in its participants at the official level, both in parties and in government. Sartre's famous example of the cafe waiter indicates the extent of the self-deception that bad faith involves:

he is playing at *being* a waiter in a café. ... The game is a kind of marking out and investigation. The child plays with his body in order to explore it, to take inventory of it; the waiter in the café plays with his condition in order to *realize* it. This obligation is not different from that which is imposed on all tradesmen. Their condition is wholly one of ceremony.[5]

Roquentin too is wrestling with the same condition in his role as a historian, his inability to resolve that triggering his recurrent state of nausea. Apply this to politics and it soon becomes clear how many politicians are merely playing at being politicians, and governments at being governments. All in a very cavalier fashion which shows considerable disdain for the public: the chaotic state of the Conservative Party government in the UK from the Covid pandemic through to its defeat in the 2024 election indicating just how cavalier. In democracies the public have been led to expect higher standards than this and to believe that they can place trust in what their politicians are saying; a trust, however, that is being severely tested in the current political climate, where charisma is coming to carry far more weight than argument does. Anyone who has ever worked at a trade or in a menial occupation will know only too well what Sartre means when he says that bad faith is imposed on them by the need to earn a living. To avoid admitting that to oneself by letting the role take you over, moulding your character to fit the system's requirements, can be seen as a defence mechanism, and that reaction can surely be sympathised with—it is a fate that many of us have had to go through, and indeed the norm for most of the population for most of their lives. Politicians, however, cannot be forgiven so easily, since they choose their career quite freely, it is not an imposition that socio-economic circumstances force on them, as it does with unfortunate waiters, etc.

How much the average politician really does believe in what they are saying when performing their ceremonial role is, however, a moot point—becoming more so as we move to the far right of the political spectrum, where rabble-rousing rhetoric and sloganeering take over from logical argument, and good faith is in notably short supply. There is a party line to be followed for professional politicians and that is what they are expected to present to the public. With an eye to their career most do, which constitutes bad faith on their part, a reaction which is never going to be in the spirit of liberal democracy. As Sartre puts it, 'in bad faith it is from myself that I am hiding the truth', and the far-right politicians I am referring to can certainly be accused of that—as can all conspiracists.[6] Sartre describes this activity as a case of 'establishing that I am not what I am', the effect of which amounts to a denial that I can be held to account by others for my actions or beliefs:

> If I were only what I am, I could, for example, seriously consider an adverse criticism which someone makes of me, question myself scrupulously, and perhaps be compelled to recognise the truth in it. But thanks to transcendence, I am not subject to all that I am. I do not even have to discuss the justice of the reproach.[7]

It is certainly true of both the politicians and conspiracists in question that they feel under no obligation to respond to any reproach at all of their conduct (you could wait for an eternity for Donald Trump or Vladimir Putin to apologise for anything they have done, one suspects). 'The goal of bad faith … is to put oneself out of reach; it is an escape', and anyone making that choice ought to be held to account for it, because what they are trying to escape from above all is responsibility—most crucially their responsibility to others (as well as performing their public role ethically).[8] It is part of this mind-set that such individuals cannot imagine that their own view of themselves might not be shared by others (or refuse to imagine it anyway). There is an intense self-centredness to this outlook which enables the individual to hold on to their beliefs as if there was no alternative; and in a democracy there always is an alternative, that is one of its defining features, as is being open to considering its possibilities for development. Not agreeing with the alternative is one thing, denying that it exists is something altogether more sinister in a democratic framework: in effect, a denial of its operating principles, as accepted and followed by both the left and the right.

Going back to the discussion on global capitalism above, it can also be said of its major players that at best most of them are just pretending to be acting with the greater public good in mind, with democracy clearly losing out from that policy as well. That would be to give some of them the benefit of the doubt, which may or may not be reasonable to assume—depends how cynical you consider global capitalists to be, I would think. At worst, however, they have managed to convince themselves that they really are, all but losing their identity in bad faith, either unable, or unwilling, to conceive of other interpretations of reality than their own: 'as a being which is what it is not and which is not what it is'.[9] That is bad faith at its most dangerous, since acceptance of it on your part could excuse just about any action you might take that would ignore the rights of others;

they just would not figure in your calculations. (Donald Trump regularly taunts the American public in this way, arguing that his supporters would continue to vote for him regardless of what he did—even up to the point of shooting someone in full view of others. Even worse, he might be right. One has to wonder what his opponents could possibly do in response to such an event.)

Although it should not be that way, politics is to many a route to personal power and prestige rather than a means of performing public service; although all will claim it is the latter, and only the latter, that motivates them, especially in their election campaigns. Yet another instance of cavalier behaviour on the part of many of them, therefore, as one suspects they will know somewhere inside themselves, but have become skilled at hiding (or as Sartre describes the complexity of this state, 'it is precisely as the acceptance of not believing what it believes that it is bad faith'[10]). There are exceptions to this rule; some politicians are not playing such games with us, but displaying their true beliefs and their firm commitment to them in a manner that can elicit trust. Willing also to consider criticism, and if need be to act on it to modify their position. That qualifies as authentic politics, and it is what most of us are looking for in our representatives; politics minus bad faith, as bad faith at this level can affect all of us adversely (as it did so dramatically during the Covid pandemic, when far too many politicians worldwide were found to be playing at being politicians when circumstances would not allow this to be covered up, casualty statistics catching up with them no matter how much they tried to excuse them away). Unfortunately, unauthenticity is far more in evidence in political life and bad faith the norm, with all too many professional politicians more than prepared to say whatever will help them get elected, even if this strays off, as it so often does these days into lies and fabrications, such as that we are being invaded by hordes of illegal immigrants; that there is an active campaign to replace the white race in Western countries by the various others determined to dominate them for their own advantage; that there is a secret deep-state operation to restrict the far right's ability to express itself and thus win elections; that climate change is a sham devised by self-interested groups in the scientific world, etc., etc. We are becoming all too familiar with these tired arguments, but they keep being trotted out so they must be having the desired effect on some, telling them what they want to know rather than what actually is the case. Other interpretations just do not exist in that universe, so self-recovery from them never really comes up as an issue. That the end justifies the means is bad faith in totally unapologetic action, and the recourse to alternative facts, and claims of being the victim of fake news, certainly merit that description. Playing the victim rather than the aggressor in this manner is yet another well-worn tactic of the far right, a particularly unsubtle version of 'establishing that I am not what I am'; a ploy designed to put oneself out of reach of judgement or any chance of reproach from others.

Politics is therefore becoming more and more a game of constructing whatever narrative suits your ends, no matter how fictional or far-fetched it may be: if it draws in an audience that is all that counts.[11] Thus immigrants can be blamed for whatever goes wrong in a Western society because a market has been built up for scapegoating of that nature. (It is striking to note in this context as well how immigrants have become the far right's new all-purpose scapegoat, taking over the role allotted to the Jews in Nazi mythology, although anti-semitism has still not gone away by any means. Eugenics is making a comeback in political discussion circles as well, being pushed by the 'remigration' movement that is becoming very vocal in the West, dredging up some of the very worst aspects of nationalism in its wake in the process.) Authoritarians are skilled at the practice and in pitching it convincingly to their public, generally presenting themselves as the only one capable of saving their country from imminent disaster. Donald Trump has been a past-master at this over the years, and leaves a potentially dangerous legacy for future generations of unscrupulous politicians willing to use all the dark arts available to their profession. (In effect, this is what Jacques Derrida in *Specters of Marx* dubs a 'hauntology', a condition that can linger on in a culture indefinitely, as it does for example with Karl Marx.[12] This being, again, a good or a bad outcome depending on your ideological position, especially since it can also be said, much more problematically, of such figures as Hitler and Mussolini.) Bad faith is for demagogues a way of life—and a very successful one too when it comes to solidifying their political power base. They do not have to consider criticism at all; they just know they are right, a conviction which they pass on to their supporters, ensnaring them in bad faith as well. This is politics as authorship as it were, to be judged by its effect rather than its relationship to reality, exactly as applies with literary fiction: truth matters less than popularity. It is the same consideration that has generated such infamous texts as *The Protocols of the Elders of Zion*:[13] a grim example of politically motivated fiction that has done endless harm down the years, inspiring many anti-semitic political movements such as the Nazis. Creative writing misused would be about the kindest comment one could make in such cases.

Political analysts would be well advised to brush up on their narratology skills in order to work out what it is that their objects of study are trying to achieve. Quest narratives feature prominently in narratology (as famously in the work of the Russian formalist Vladimir Propp[14]), each with a distinctive narrative arc, which suggests that we ought to be finding out just what kind of quest narrative is being set up by political campaigners, and to what expected end, if we want to deflect it and limit the damage it could cause. Granted, all ideologies are narratives of one kind or another, claiming to offer the route to a better lifestyle if their proposals are followed; but the extent to which they relate to factual evidence becomes crucial. Lying simply does not, it is just one more piece of fiction, thus a matter for aesthetics rather than politics (an issue I will be returning to). It tends to generate rather boring and repetitive fiction too. Yet lying all too often works on a receptive audience (which demagogues attract as a matter of course), sad though that state of affairs is for any liberal democracy; they can all become, as I put it earlier, ensnared in bad faith, seeing this as reality. When narratives in effect invent their own evidence—again, something Donald Trump has perfected as a political tactic, categorising him as an author instead of a politician in the stricter sense, if not a particularly subtle or original one it should be said—then democracies are in real trouble. They will continue to be as well as long as we are bombarded by such fantasies of defiantly ill intent; creative writing does not deserve such misuse, and literary criticism will not suffice to point out its flaws. We find ourselves in the realm of intractable differends once more, where politics has a tendency to break down, differends and debate being totally incompatible entities. A differend is a negation of debate, which serves far-right politicians only too well in their campaign to restrict the public sphere, all the better to control it for their own benefit. Differends are also an open invitation to bad faith, since there is no admission by the parties involved that another interpretation of events is even possible: tunnel vision applies instead and that is a specialty of the far right.

Politics, Aesthetics and Authoritarianism

Coming back to the subject of aesthetics versus politics, it is worth noting that this was an issue which came to the fore in the 1930s, when the Nazis very deliberately, and it has to be admitted very effectively, turned politics into a form of theatre—as in the notorious Nuremberg rallies, for example, with their elaborately choreographed sequences designed to rouse a crowd to hysterical fervour for their leader and his ideology. That is a prominent aspect of the background in which Sartre is composing *Nausea*. It is a precedent which should raise alarm in an era of fake news and alternative facts. When aesthetics and politics overlap in this manner the public is in grave danger of being manipulated in a democratically unacceptable fashion (the deployment of AI by the unscrupulous can only make the situation worse, as we are only just beginning to find out). Fiction is, and should remain, a critically important part of our lives (I say this as someone who has spent a large part of their academic career teaching the subject), but its infiltration into the realm of politics is a flagrant misuse of its life-affirming qualities. It is one thing to take *Nausea* as a point of comparison for what is happening now socio-politically and see if the novel helps us put this into some kind of perspective that can shape our response as authentically as we can, quite another to assume that your own made-up narrative is a true account of what is happening. Furthermore, an account which is to be considered beyond debate or any sort of rational analysis; it is what it is because you say that it is, and no other explanation is needed—nor will be offered. Narrative can work for good or ill in that respect, can be used or abused. The riots that broke out in various UK cities in the summer of 2024 were all based on an entirely false narrative about immigrants, posted on the net predictably, indicating just how dangerous this practice has the capacity to be. That constitutes an inexcusable abuse of narrative, and it is one that we need to be constantly on the lookout for in the political domain, especially now that it has managed to entrench itself so deeply there.

If the likes of Trump are authors then they are authors of whom we should be very wary indeed. Vladimir Putin can be placed in the same category, given his baseless justification for invading Ukraine being that it was to free it from fascist rulers; another case of narrative masquerading as fact for ulterior motives—in this instance a wish to recreate the Russian empire that was, with Putin as a de facto czar. Recreating empires is one of the most insidious of political narratives, if also, unfortunately enough, one that can still generate a significant amount of popular appeal, especially when touted by a strong man leader: think Mussolini and his attempt to establish a new Roman empire, for instance. Bringing back a supposedly glorious past is always a dubious project, one that will rarely stand up to very much scrutiny: glorious for whom, and for what reasons, being critical considerations that its proponents simply gloss over. Political empires always involve a great deal of the absurd in their operation and the nostalgia they can create is invariably misplaced, exploitation of people and resources being conveniently forgotten—plus the authoritarianism needed to police such systems that so often leaves ex-colonies with long-running social problems that can hold back their development for generations afterwards (Africa in particular is full of just such examples to this day). Trump's MAGA cult uses much the same methodology, so perhaps we could add false nostalgia to the list of things that should raise alarm in a post-truth world; truth being hidden in this way is never likely to end well. In each case narratives are being deployed to deceive us as to the aims of their authoritarian-minded narrators, which inevitably will be in their own interest not that of the wider public, a discrepancy they are incapable of recognising since they assume their viewpoint is the only one that ever counts on any matter. Democracy should be steering well clear of such nostalgia and those who peddle it as if it were some kind of received truth instead of just mere belief. As Sartre sums it up: 'Bad faith is belief; and the essential problem of bad faith is a problem of belief'.[15] Hence the need for scepticism to call into question the grounds, if any, for such belief—and scepticism is not a trait to be found in authoritarianism. Nor is it a trait to be found in climate-crisis sceptics or fossil-fuel producers either, as I will go on to discuss next.

Notes

1. Jean-François Lyotard, *The Differend: Phrases in Dispute* (1983), trans. Georges Van Den Abbeele, Manchester: Manchester University Press, 1988.
2. Jean-Paul Sartre, *Iron in the Soul* (1949), trans. Gerard Hopkins, London: Penguin, 2002.
3. Jean-Paul Sartre, *The Reprieve* (1945), trans. Eric Sutton, London: Penguin, 1986, p. 75.
4. Anne Applebaum, *Autocracy, Inc.: The Dictators Who Want to Run the World*, New York and London: Allen Lane, 2024, p. 2.
5. Jean-Paul Sartre, *Being and Nothingness: An Essay on Phenomenological Ontology* (1943), trans. Hazel E. Barnes, London: Methuen, 1958, p. 59.
6. Ibid., p. 49.
7. Ibid., p. 57.
8. Ibid., p. 65.
9. Ibid., p. 58.
10. Ibid., p. 70.

11. Donald Trump's claim, made in a televised 2024 presidential debate, that Haitian immigrants to America were capturing and eating family cats and dogs might well go down as the low point of this tendency to date. No doubt variants of this will circulate around the conspiracy theory network for years to come.
12. See Jacques Derrida, *Specters of Marx: The State of the Debt, the Work of Mourning, and the New International* (1993), trans Peggy Kamuf, New York and London: Routledge, 1994, p. 10.
13. Although exposed as a fraud as long ago as 1921 in *The Times* newspaper, the text can still be found on the net if you choose to hunt around for it (and obviously many do). As I note at several points in the text, conspiracy theories never really die out.
14. See, for example, Vladimir Propp, *The Morphology of the Folktale*, trans. Laurence Scott, Austin, TX and London, University of Texas Press, 1958.
15. Sartre, *Being and Nothingness*, p. 67.

References

Applebaum, Anne, *Autocracy, Inc.: The Dictators Who Want to Run the World*, New York and London: Allen Lane, 2024.

Derrida, Jacques, *Specters of Marx: The State of the Debt, the Work of Mourning, and the New International* (1993), trans Peggy Kamuf, New York and London: Routledge, 1994.

Lyotard, Jean-François, *The Differend: Phrases in Dispute* (1983), trans. Georges Van Den Abbeele, Manchester: Manchester University Press, 1988.

Propp, Vladimir, *The Morphology of the Folktale*, trans. Laurence Scott, Austin, TX and London, University of Texas Press, 1958.

Sartre, Jean-Paul, *Nausea* (1938), trans. Robert Baldick, Harmondsworth: Penguin, 1965.

———. *Being and Nothingness: An Essay on Phenomenological Ontology* (1943), trans. Hazel E. Barnes, London: Methuen, 1958.

———. *The Reprieve* (1945), trans. Eric Sutton, London: Penguin, 1986.

———. *Iron in the Soul*, (1949), trans. Gerard Hopkins, London: Penguin, 2002.

CHAPTER 3

Climate Crisis

Abstract Climate crisis, plus the arguments around it, is investigated in this chapter, as is the generally very weak response to this all-important issue by most governments. The fossil-fuel industry is criticised for its denial of the problem its product is causing, and its obsession with gaining the most profit it can at the expense of any environmental concerns. Bad faith is much in evidence in the corporate response to climate crisis, as it is in the political, which heavily prioritises economic growth over environmental considerations when it comes to electioneering. Existentialism is argued to promote a 'collective conscience' against market-driven choices, such as the use of private cars rather than mass public transport, and to encourage us to develop a less consumerist culture than is currently the case. The need for more authenticity in the public response to climate crisis is emphasised.

Keywords Climate crisis • Authoritarianism • Bad faith • Conspiracy theory • Anthropocene • Jean-Paul Sartre • Existentialism • Authenticity • Fossil fuel • Consumerism

Self-deception and bad faith loom very large again when it comes to climate crisis, constituting an even more existential threat to the human race than does political authoritarianism. For most of us in the West it is the overwhelmingly critical issue of our age, becoming noticeably more critical year by year as well. Yet it can seem as if the powers-that-be, both political and corporate, strong leaders prominently active among them, are determined to see just how far they can test the limits of the environment in their relentless search for power and profits. The regular Assessment Reports put out by the Intergovernmental Panel on Climate Change (IPCC) make it only too clear how dangerous a game this is proving to be, with each sounding even more alarming than the last when it comes to phenomena such as sea-level rises (melting 'doomsday' polar glaciers playing their part). Yet climate crisis denial is actively promoted by the vested interests in the fossil-fuel industry despite what is now an overwhelming amount of evidence that the problem is running out of our control; that we are rapidly heading for the dreaded tipping-points that scientists keep warning us about, from which there will be no return to normality. The latter are no longer so much of a projection as an actual reality that is having a dramatic effect on weather patterns globally, with storms, heatwaves, wildfires, rainfall, and droughts intensifying on an unprecedented scale that is already stretching emergency services to their limits across the world. Hurricanes, as a case in point, are regularly wreaking havoc on the eastern seaboard in America and the Caribbean region, causing dramatic mass evacuations, as in autumn 2024's Helene and Milton, and these are being forecast to become ever stronger and more frequent as climate crisis progresses.

Certain parts of the world are in danger of turning into no-go areas if such trends are allowed to continue unchecked, but even that would probably not be enough to silence the denialist lobby and their funders. Climate scientists see patterns in such events that point to the impact of carbon emissions on the atmosphere, so theoretically reversible if appropriate action were to be taken—preferably starting right away. Denialists, on the other hand, see one-offs that could not have been prevented, mere accidents of nature as it were. There is no common ground between them, with a huge gap in how evidence is interpreted.

Denial is also a specialty of the conspiracy theory community, meaning that examples of it as regards the climate are constantly circulating on social media, there to be picked up by the unwary and impressionable. It is in fact the name of the game for this community, which will deny anything and everything that does not fit with their beliefs, these being in effect set in stone; it is, as I suggested before, the very basis of their ideology, and of the bad faith that drives it. Authenticity is never going to be thought of or discussed in such circles, which refuses to admit that there is anything to recover from. For such a mentality, climate change is an invented problem and to be denounced as such, particularly any campaign to reach net zero with carbon emissions, which is treated as an unnecessary burden on the economy dreamed up by the politically naive and meddlesome. Even the notion of an Anthropocene age, where it is human activity that is taken to be shaping the development of the environment, now a widely accepted concept amongst scientists, can be denied by such zealots (who can include, worryingly enough, many senior politicians in their ranks). Yet the proliferation of terms the condition is generating—climate change/emergency/crisis/disaster/breakdown/boiling, for example—is enough to bring on a state of nausea in anyone who reflects on it seriously. Perhaps barbecue might be the ultimate fate awaiting the human race?

Most governments internationally claim to be in favour of reducing carbon emissions, but when it comes to positive action to achieve this goal, they tend to keep it to a minimum because of the costs involved—as well as the threat it might pose to their country's economic growth. The latter factor is still the overriding concern of almost all democratic political parties (the Greens being the only notable exception, although they rarely get into positions of power to put their theories into practice), endlessly paraded in election manifestos and campaigns as if its validity were entirely self-evident. The downsides of growth, such as that it will always put further strain on an already dangerously over-strained environment, are rarely mentioned by the major participants. That is considered to be electoral poison; definitely something to be hidden, both from oneself and others. In most cases dealing with the problem is postponed to a later date, with vague promises to 'transition' away from dependence on fossil-fuel power over a period of decades. That is a timescale, however, which takes no account of the speed at which the process is occurring, taking such entities as the retreating Thwaites glacier along with it (and you can be sure there will be others to follow, most likely sooner rather than later as well).

Even this decision is only grudgingly supported by those countries with large reserves of oil and gas, such as Saudi Arabia and Russia, which have a vested interest in maintaining the current system as long as they possibly can, given that their economy is heavily structured on this. More vague, and generally unfulfilled, promises to work towards net zero are most likely going to be the pattern here, especially since little happens when such targets are not kept—except that some new, very much notional, schedule for reduction is put forward (COP conferences are becoming notorious for just such empty resolutions, to the despair of environmentalists everywhere). One has to suspect that President Trump will not even bother to offer that kind of sop to public opinion, as he is an adamant climate change denier committed to increasing America's oil production and as such deaf to any complaints from environmentalists. Profit yet again wins out therefore, being allowed to swamp all other considerations: capitalism is entirely predictable on that score and will remain so, that is simply its nature. Neither is changing the dynamics of that system going to be a concern of much note to the far right.

It can feel as if we are collectively sleep-walking into a disaster, and the extent of the bad faith involved needs to be called out repeatedly. The argument here will build upon recent studies on the existentialist implications of climate crisis by such commentators as Matthew C. Ally, Paul Gyllenhammer, and Markus Moos, reassessing these in terms of what is a constantly, and rapidly, changing situation. We are all in the Anthropocene, whether or not we happen to like it, and it is unauthentic to refuse to acknowledge the fact; denial does not work against natural phenomena. We are all also in what climate scientists are now calling 'ecological overshoot', meaning that we are straining the Earth's resources more than it has the capacity to restore itself from—and doing that on a systematic basis. That is a trend that can only end badly, whatever denialists may say or believe. We certainly cannot expect the Earth to recover on its own if we keep corrupting its systems on a grand scale; authenticity demands that we do our utmost to create the conditions on which any such recovery could be possible. Chaos theory warns us that failure to do so is to expose our environmental system to the threat of collapsing altogether, and no amount of plans to colonise Mars will save us from that. Chaos spells the end of self-recovery anywhere.

Profit Versus Climate

As noted above, it is profit that dictates the response to climate change when it comes to the fossil-fuel industry and its supporters. The profits involved can, by the standards of the bulk of the population, approach the obscene as well, running into billions of dollars a year with really big players such as the major oil companies (accompanied of course by appropriately high annual bonuses for top executives and bumper dividends for shareholders, keeping them complicit). Shell Oil has posted profits of $28 billion for 2023, followed up by $14 billion in the first half of 2024, and there are many other oil companies around the world cashing in on this reliably buoyant trade. Figures like that do not encourage any altruistic revision of one's business priorities; indeed they actively militate against it. Greed can never be discounted as a factor in such situations, and that just has to qualify as bad faith—if also, unhelpfully, a very widespread trait throughout our money-obsessed societies. The occasional windfall tax has little overall effect on the industry either, given that it can always rearrange its pricing to cover these and keep its shareholders content. Authenticity is not much in play anywhere in this area, and never likely to be if the industry is left to its own devices, as neoliberal economics, with its outright rejection of the need for any governmental regulation, insists all business organisations should be. It is the obsession with the non-interventionist small state concept that lies behind such thinking, revealing its anti-democratic, and more than somewhat anarchistic, cast.

There was a period back in the 1990s when the projection was that we were reaching, and could even be said to have reached, peak oil, and that supplies would begin to dwindle if global energy use went on growing at the rate it was then doing. That should have been a point of reflection as to where this was all heading and whether it should be allowed to continue on unchecked, and it did to an extent encourage something of a move internationally into green energy production. Since then, however, the fossil-fuel industry has become increasingly efficient at finding as yet untapped sites to develop, no matter how inaccessible or dangerous these may prove to be, thus managing to keep meeting even a growing demand. The Arctic has become a major area of interest, for example, even though any large-scale exploitation of the resources there very easily could threaten an already delicate environmental balance on which the world's climate critically depends. The addiction to profit, however, overrules all objections as far as the industry's giants go; short-term benefits being given precedence over any longer-term threat to the environment. That is simply the way our economic system operates, the short-term will always dominate in the market's mind, and what the market wants the market will get one way or another. Shareholders want investments to maximise their returns now, not at some notional point in the future that could be delayed by government action on emissions, and will seek out appropriate places to achieve that: the market is a law unto itself in that respect.

The environment is to be considered someone else's concern, therefore, not the market's—or the business world's in general come to that, which is free to ignore what the various climate summits organised by the United Nations recommend urgently needs to be done if the crisis is going to be addressed seriously. That is not a basis on which to combat climate change, but it is what we are currently stuck with and will have to find ways around. Once again we are faced by a choice between cynicism and bad faith in trying to work out the state of mind behind such conduct, which plainly is not in the wider public interest—and never will be. It can sometimes seem as if the market and business world approach to climate crisis is at the level of crossing one's fingers and hoping it will just go away (then forgetting about it for as long as one is allowed to). This hardly encourages the rest of the population to think any differently, so things just tend to drift on much as before with fuel consumption constantly increasing, just as the fossil-fuel industry would want it to go on doing in perpetuity.

The obsession with economic growth, by Western nations in particular, means that carbon emissions are inevitably going to keep on rising in volume, because energy expenditure will continue to do so. Green energy will go some way towards ameliorating this, as will carbon capture schemes, which several governments have begun to invest in of late. The latter can be very expensive to run, however, making politicians wary of adopting them on any large scale in case that requires tax rises to cover the cost (and tax rises definitely qualify as electoral poison in the West). So far they have had little impact on the overall emissions total, and would need to be magnified considerably as an operation to do so. But as long as there is profit to be made, and that is the only thing that will attract large-scale market investment, then fossil fuel will be turned to as the easy way to speed growth up. It is straightforward for consumers to access and there are large stocks of it available, plus a system designed to deliver it on a reliable basis (as in the many pipelines traversing the globe). Pushing growth along as fast as possible is something that politicians will always want to facilitate, given that it is going to be one of their main calling cards in the next election: not one of democracy's more appealing traits.

There is a degrowth movement making a compelling case against this lifestyle, as in the work of Serge Latouche,[1] and while it has its intellectual followers few of them are in the professional political class of the democratic world, so its message goes largely unheeded (most politicians and economists treat it as at best a niche concern, of interest only to naive idealists). Politics tends to be remorselessly short-term in its outlook in that respect. No matter what might be said about imminent boiling, etc., a forthcoming election will invariably render this a relatively low priority for discussion amongst the main political parties; generally sidelined as an issue to be dealt with at some future point. Growth will always dominate on such occasions as this is what the public has been programmed to expect, not a detailed discussion on how we should respond to the latest IPCC Assessment Report. That is yet another narrative which urgently needs to be re-examined: IPCC Reports really *ought* to be an election issue, not whether, as the catchphrase so often goes in American presidential elections, 'do you feel better off than you did four years ago?'. Questions like that trivialise the democratic process, which really ought to be far more sophisticated than that. At some point in the not too distant future the question really ought to become, 'do you feel more safe against climate crisis than you did four years ago?'.

The effect of such self-interested political decisions, plus the persistence of what could be dubbed Climate Crisis Denial Inc., means that many individuals can end up taking refuge in bad faith, hiding the truth of the situation from themselves because it all seems so far out of their control (conspiracy theory offering a convenient bolt-hole if you want a more manageable explanation for why things have gone wrong, and who to blame for it). Understandable though that reaction is—bad faith by default as it were—it has to be campaigned against, and vigorously. At some point it will not be possible to apologise for being slow to take action and to promise to change our ways: that cannot be said often enough. Melting polar icecaps cannot be replaced (even if some claims have been made that geoengineering might help to slow this down[2]). Neither will conspiracy theory save us from dramatically rising sea levels or the climate extremes that cause these. Analyses that once seemed apocalyptically sensationalist in their claims (James Lovelock's *The Revenge of Gaia*, for example, or Mark Lynas's *Six Degrees*), are beginning to seem more like the inevitable fate awaiting us all as governments dither about how, or even whether, to respond to the changes being logged all around us by the IPCC et al. Lovelock predicts that if we go on as we are then 'only a handful of the teeming billions now alive will survive', and they would be restricted to eking out a basic existence in the Arctic as the only habitable place left on Earth.[3] Lynas details the environmental changes that would take place with every added degree on Earth's average temperature from its pre-Industrial Revolution base, leading well before reaching the top end of 6 to 'the worst of all earthly outcomes: mass extinction'.[4] We have now reached the 1.5 mark and are already struggling to cope, as well as continuing to move ever upwards. Meanwhile every passing year seems to be on course to being the hottest ever recorded, but obviously that cannot go on indefinitely without generating environmental catastrophe on a scale that none of us could hope to escape from. We really are all in this together and no part of the world is safe from being affected; extreme weather events can happen anywhere, on any continent, in any country, at any time of year. Climate crisis fatigue is an understandable reaction to all of this, but that would be to lapse into bad faith yet again; committed campaigning just has to continue, regardless of how many obstacles bad faith puts in the way, as is its wont.

Some scientists are beginning to argue that it is legitimate to allow appeals to the emotion to come into play in such campaigning, on the grounds that this might jolt us out of climate crisis fatigue and the apathy that it fosters. Their point, outlined in an article in the journal *Nature Climate Change*, is that it is no longer possible to be objective about the breakdown of the natural systems around us, that it has to be made clear this is not just an intellectual exercise of collecting and publishing data then hoping that someone in power happens to notice and act on it.[5] Rather than trusting to luck in that fashion, we should in fact be worried and fearful and communicating those feelings as loudly as we can in an effort to generate a more determined response to the crisis by governments worldwide, since merely putting the scientific data out there in the public domain is not having that desired effect. While there is an air of desperation to such appeals, they also help to humanise the issue, emphasising again that we really are all in this together, both climate scientists and lay public. Perhaps we need to add desperation to the pessimism that *New Scientist* recommends as a useful way of approaching the issue constructively? Given the circumstances it would be more realistic than simply hoping for the best, or assuming that things will somehow or other turn out all right in the longer term, because at the moment climate science is giving us little reason to feel that way.

Existentialism and the Public Good

Existentialism readily lends itself to debates about the public good, as can be seen in Markus Moos's study of traffic management in North American cities such as Toronto, an issue which sets individual against general public in a particularly stark manner. The extent of pollution from city traffic is well known and much commented upon and complained about, cars being the dominant feature of almost every cityscape (plus the packed roads and traffic jams they create). In an abstract way most of the public would probably want it to be reduced to improve the quality of everyday life; as public health officials keep telling us, it is the cause of many deaths around the globe that tougher legislation could bring down quite substantially. When such a move is made, however, it soon comes into conflict with the average driver's wishes to be allowed to go wherever they want, whenever they want (and as quickly as they want too). The Conservative Party in the UK even claimed during the 2024 election campaign that such schemes (as in designated low-emission zones that had been set up in several UK cities, with reduced-speed limits to back them up) amounted to a 'war on motorists'—emotive language which attracted quite a bit of support and media coverage (from the usual suspects, who did not think to wonder whether this might better have been called a 'war on polluters'). Car-use is almost seen as some kind of divine right in the West (by drivers certainly), and any restrictions placed on this activity, even when manifestly for the general public good, as low-emission zones can surely claim to be, are likely to stir up protest in the driving community. A minor such alteration in my own neighbourhood recently led to a local councillor losing their seat, an outcome which could happen anywhere and of which politicians in general are always fearful, leading many of them to be very cautious about their involvement in such schemes. It is far easier to lose than to gain votes on such plans in urban areas, meaning it then becomes a case of yes, it is a good idea but just not here, and certainly not now while I am still in office. As with the adverse effects of economic growth, it is an issue where kicking the can down the road is a popular response, leaving it a problem for someone else to deal with ideally. That is yet another game that cannot go on indefinitely either without having some really serious side effects.

Almost all action on climate change by the authorities, whether at national or international level, soon comes up against a similar collision of interests: a collision that the fossil-fuel industry is only too happy to foster in pursuit of their own ends. Yet another case of 'freedom from' and 'freedom to' in conflict, as they so often are. As far as the latter is concerned the less action taken over climate change the better (nothing at all would be their preferred option, shamefully enough) and the general public good does not enter into that calculation. The environment is again to be considered someone else's problem, not the corporate world's, which is never going to be in favour of any regulation that curbs its sales. That, and profit, is where their belief lies, which means they are always going to be on the side of growth and promoting it where they can, financially and otherwise (every new oilfield will be sold to the local populations on the basis of what it will do for their economy, creating more jobs, etc., a line which generally works as intended in winning the general public over).

Moos argues that existentialism assumes a 'collective conscience', that can be made to work against market-driven choices by individuals, with their more selfish implications.[6] If the latter are allowed to dominate, then the situation as regards pollution will only keep deteriorating. 'We built our cities around the car', as Moos points out, 'So it would only seem fair that we should now make provisions for those that choose alternate ways of getting around'.[7] He goes on to argue that we should turn to existentialism for help in changing our assumptions about urban traffic, because it 'emphasizes the dynamic between individual choice and collective impacts'—'freedom to' and 'freedom from' in differend-style confrontation at this point. The problem with most politics on the right is that it is fixated on the former at the expense of the latter, which weighs heavily in favour of individual car-use, and cities, particularly large ones, need far less of that rather than yet more. Those who follow that line of thought are acting in bad faith in terms of the wider public interest. How they interpret 'freedom' can be a crucial marker in determining an individual's susceptibility to bad faith, as can its effect on others when put into action. Moos sums it up neatly when he suggests that '[e]xistentialism may provide a new(ish) philosophical justification for why people should care about the collective in an age of growing individualism'.[8] They should, but that is not a characteristic associated with culture warriors.

Paul Gyllenhammer also makes a strong case for existentialism's importance as an analytical method to apply to issues such as climate change. When it comes to traffic pollution, for example, individuals can come to recognise 'the environmental responsibility of mass transit'.[9] Everyone using that system would then be displaying authentic behaviour for a common good: the 'collective consciousness' that Moos identifies as critical for addressing such problems effectively. Collective impact should always be kept in mind when individuals are deciding where their responsibility lies. Freedom to put others' health at risk by the choices you make—as, for example, in the case of transportation (smoking is another area raising similar concerns)—would hardly qualify as acting responsibly from an existentialist viewpoint. What we ought to be displaying in such situations is what Gyllenhammer dubs 'relational respect'.[10] That reveals itself 'only when we pay heed to the reckless power we wield over beings that deserve our respect' (both human and non-human, as Gyllenhammer insists).[11] That is not behaviour we can expect from the far right, however: reckless power is exactly what they want to wield over all others, given that they do not really respect the rights of any who think differently to them. Authoritarianism in general is obsessed with power, and will use it to close down anyone that opposes it, whether on environmental issues or anything else; relational respect is highly unlikely to be on its agenda either.

Ally's objective is to establish a role for existentialism within contemporary ecological concerns, while admitting that Sartre himself is not the most obvious candidate for such a task. As Ally remarks: 'it is well known, after all, that he did not particularly like nature' (Roquentin does not seem all that drawn to nature either, as I will be discussing later).[12] A significant amount of stretching and bending is required to make this exercise work therefore, but once again it is the resonance and suggestiveness of Sartre's concepts that are the important considerations to bear in mind, not what Sartre himself said about nature as such (if not always helpful for ecological commentators, it has to be remembered just how recent the recognition of, and widespread public concern over, climate change as a life-threatening problem actually is; Sartre largely precedes this, so can be granted some leeway). Whether or not we can claim an ecological consciousness in Sartre's work (Ally thinks we can, if a qualified one) is of less interest in this study than how we can adapt his concepts to a range of pressing socio-political problems that are currently bedevilling us. Sartre's views on nature do not affect the validity or utility of concepts like bad faith, which, bearing in mind Roland Barthes's notion of 'the death of the author', must be assumed to take on a life of their own once they are out in the general world of ideas.[13] Ally feels the need to address the various problematic aspects in Sartre's thought as regards ecology before deploying his thought in that direction, and he makes an interesting case in that respect. These will not be a concern of mine here, however; the concepts can stand alone, to be judged by their use-value.

For the editors of *Earthly Engagements* we are in the midst of 'a *planetary socioecological crisis*', and the book offers a range of views and approaches as to how existentialism can help us address this daunting challenge.[14] Above all what an existentialist response requires is 'collective action', and the point of the book is to suggest several ways this can be realised.[15] One of these is through consumerism, an area where various contributors find bad faith to be a deeply entrenched problem that requires urgent attention. As Elizabeth Butterfield persuasively argues, '[a]t the heart of so many of the environmental crises we face today we find the over-consumption of goods. We in developed nations have more "stuff" than ever before'.[16] Nowhere is this more true than in the over-consumption of fossil fuels, which plays a critical role in the production of everything we consume—and more consumption can only mean yet more carbon emissions thus rising global temperatures. (It is fair to say that few of us think of the emission implications when a new product comes on the market or a new manufacturing technique is developed.) Quite literally, we buy into this every day of our lives in what we eat, drink and wear, making us complicit in the bad faith that is engrained in a capitalist economic system. Tourism can be added to the list as well, given how much it has expanded as an activity in recent history and how wasteful it is of resources, most notably of fossil fuels for transport.

While we are all becoming more aware of that complicity, the system traps us to a large extent as it is such an integral part of our society, taken for granted by us in our everyday lives. The political obsession with economic growth underpins it too, especially since most of the electorate in the West have been programmed, basically from their youth onwards, to agree with its aims. But there are various campaigns trying to change our habits in this area, as in the move towards plant-based foods and away from meat-heavy diets with their far greater carbon output in production terms, and these deserve all the support we can give them. Although as Butterfield warns, 'changing our behaviors will require much more than, say, choosing between paper or plastic' (or one type of food than another for that matter).[17]

Consumer culture has become a way of dealing with our existential anxieties much in the way that religion has functioned throughout history, distracting us from these for a while (if only temporarily, in the way of addictions in general), but that is to avoid the real problem. The existentialist answer has to be to become more honest with ourselves, to analyse how and why we are falling into bad faith so regularly and to work harder on achieving an authentic lifestyle, despite our anxieties (which none of us can escape from in a metaphysical sense anyway). No-one ever said this would be easy, and the barriers to doing so are becoming ever more formidable, as the growing ranks of denialists, authoritarians, and conspiracy theorists attest. If we keep facing up to them, campaigning collectively as powerfully as we can, then we might just have a chance of avoiding a worst-case scenario: if not, then we are all but inviting an extinction event. (There is an eerie premonition of what such an event might feel like to the helpless individual, in Roquentin's horrified musings about 'vast, vague Nature' at the end of his time in Bouville, having completed his history of the Marquis de Rollebon: 'I know that it has no laws, that what they consider its constancy doesn't exist. It has nothing but habits and it may change those tomorrow. What if something were to happen? What if all of a sudden it started palpitating?'.[18] As he pointedly goes on to add: 'What use would their dykes and ramparts and power-houses and furnaces and pile-drivers be to them then?'.[19] It all sounds like Lovelock's 'Revenge of Gaia', when nature moves completely outside of human control in an overwhelming act of 'ecological overshoot' from which there can be no recovery.)

Consumerism is an issue that liberal democracy will have particular difficulties resolving. It is one of its cornerstones as an ideology that it offers a higher standard of living than other political systems, as well as one designed to be constantly improving over the generations: children are supposed to feel better off than their parents, and something is wrong if they are not. That has become a major part of its contract with its citizens, and it was never questioned all that much as an objective before climate change came on the scene. Now that we are in 'a planetary socioecological crisis', however, it has to be; it is no longer just an ethical issue, it is turning into one of survival. Neither is this just a case of 'going green' in our purchases, as Michael Butler makes clear. 'Green consumerism' is, for Butler, 'a trap', in that it makes our individual choices seem far more significant than they actually are, when what we ought to be doing is engaging in collective action to alter the systemic causes of climate crisis (a recurrent note amongst existentialist commentators).[20] In other words, this is a call for larger-scale political action against our profit-biased socio-economic system and the massive damage it is doing to us all (including denialists, whether they are prepared to admit it or not); an argument for the development of 'ecologically oriented political projects', as Damon Boria puts it.[21] One thing is for certain, such projects will not be generated by authoritarian governments and their followers, nor by conspiracy theorists.

Ultimately, it is a classic existentialist quandary that we find ourselves in when it comes to the current state of the climate. It is manifestly not where we would prefer to be, but we are there nevertheless and will have to make our choices within the limits of the situation—'vast, vague Nature', as it were—sets. Authenticity has to start somewhere, and climate crisis heads the list of where it is needed most urgently right now.

Notes

1. See Serge Latouche, *Farewell to Growth* (2007), trans. David Macey, Cambridge and Malden, MA: Polity Press, 2009.
2. See, for example, Madeleine Cuff, 'Plan to Refreeze Arctic Sea Ice Shows Promise in First Tests', *New Scientist*, 28 September 2024, p. 10. The practicality of geoengineering projects, especially on this kind of scale, continues to be a controversial matter in scientific circles however, since these can have adverse unintended consequences elsewhere in the system.
3. James Lovelock, *The Revenge of Gaia: Earth's Climate Crisis and the Fate of Humanity*, London: Allen Lane, 2006, p. 189.
4. Mark Lynas, *Six Degrees: Our Future on a Hotter Planet*, London: HarperCollins, 2007, p. 223.
5. Shobha Maharaj, Gretta Peci and Lisa Schipper, 'Scientists Have Emotional Responses to Climate Change Too', *Nature Climate Change* 14(10), October 2024.
6. Markus Moos, 'Existentialism: A Guiding Philosophy for Tackling Climate Change in Cities?', *The Conversation*, https://theconversation.com/existentialism-a-guiding-philosophy-for-tackling-climate-change-in-cities (accessed 12 November, 2024).
7. Ibid.
8. Ibid.
9. Paul Gyllenhammer, 'Sartre and Heidegger on Social Deformation and the Anthropocene', *Sartre Studies International*, 24:2, 2018, pp. 25–44 (p. 36).
10. Ibid., p. 25.
11. Ibid., p. 26.
12. Matthew C. Ally, *Ecology and Existence: Bringing Sartre to the Water's Edge*, Lanham, MD and London: Lexington Books, 2017, p. 25.
13. See Roland Barthes, 'The Death of the Author', in *Image Music Text*, trans. and ed. Stephen Heath, London: Fontana, 1977, pp. 142–8.
14. 'Introduction' to Matthew C. Ally and Damon Boria, eds, *Earthly Engagements: Reading Sartre After the Holocene*, Lanham, MD and London: Lexington Books, 2023, pp. 1–10 (p. 1).

15. Ibid., p. 4.
16. Elizabeth Butterfield, 'I Am What I Buy: Bad Faith and Consumer Culture', in ibid., pp. 93–121 (p. 93).
17. Ibid., p. 94.
18. Jean-Paul Sartre, *Nausea* (1938), trans. Robert Baldick, Harmondsworth: Penguin, 1965, p. 225.
19. Ibid., p. 226.
20. Michael Butler, 'Buying Green: A Trap for Fools, or, Sartre on Ethical Consumerism', in Ally and Boria, eds, *Earthly Engagements*, pp. 123–40 (p. 124).
21. See Damon Boria, 'Toward Ecologically Oriented Political Projects: Reimagining Existentialism at Algren's Cabin', in ibid., pp. 257–80.

References

Ally, Matthew C., *Ecology and Existence: Bringing Sartre to the Water's Edge*, Lanham, MD and London: Lexington Books, 2017.
———. and Damon Boria, eds, *Earthly Engagements: Reading Sartre After the Holocene*, Lanham, MD and London: Lexington Books, 2023.
Barthes, Roland, 'The Death of the Author', in *Image Music Text*, trans. and ed. Stephen Heath, London: Fontana, 1977, pp. 142–8.
Boria, Damon, 'Toward Ecologically Oriented Political Projects: Reimagining Existentialism at Algren's Cabin', in Matthew C. Ally and Damon Boria, eds, *Earthly Engagements: Reading Sartre After the Holocene*, Lanham, MD and London: Lexington Books, 2023, pp. 257–80.
Butler, Michael, 'Buying Green: A Trap for Fools, or, Sartre on Ethical Consumerism', in Matthew C. Ally and Damon Boria, eds, *Earthly Engagements: Reading Sartre After the Holocene*, Lanham, MD and London: Lexington Books, 2023, pp. 123–40.
Butterfield, Elizabeth, 'I Am What I Buy: Bad Faith and Consumer Culture', in Matthew C. Ally and Damon Boria, eds, *Earthly Engagements: Reading Sartre After the Holocene*, Lanham, MD and London: Lexington Books, 2023, pp. 93–121.
Cuff, Madeleine, 'Plan to Refreeze Arctic Sea Ice Shows Promise in First Tests', *New Scientist*, 28 September 2024, p. 10.
Gyllenhammer, Paul, 'Sartre and Heidegger on Social Deformation and the Anthropocene', *Sartre Studies International*, 24:2, 2018, pp. 25–44.
Latouche, Serge, *Farewell to Growth* (2007), trans. David Macey, Cambridge and Malden, MA: Polity Press, 2009.
Lovelock, James, *The Revenge of Gaia: Earth's Climate Crisis and the Fate of Humanity*, London: Allen Lane, 2006.

Lynas, Mark, *Six Degrees: Our Future on a Hotter Planet*, London: HarperCollins, 2007.

Maharaj, Shobha, Gretta Peci and Lisa Schipper, 'Scientists Have Emotional Responses to Climate Change Too', *Nature Climate Change* 14(10), October 2024.

Moos, Markus, 'Existentialism: A Guiding Philosophy for Tackling Climate Change in Cities?', *The Conversation*, https://theconversation.com/existentialism-a-guiding-philosophy-for-tackling-climate-change-in-cities (accessed 12 November, 2024).

Sartre, Jean-Paul, *Nausea* (1938), trans. Robert Baldick, Harmondsworth: Penguin, 1965.

CHAPTER 4

Universal Theories

Abstract The detrimental effect that universal theories (or, theories of everything) have on geopolitics is the topic of this chapter. Their tendency to substitute faith for reason is criticised, as it represents a threat to the democratic ethos, privileging dogmatism over debate. Conspiracy theory is seen to involve a similar mind-set and therefore to hold dangers for democracy as well. Marxism is taken to be a classic example of a universal theory, and Jean-Paul Sartre's critical response to it over his career is discussed, as in his critique of communism in *What Is Literature?* The impact of universal theories in religion (monotheisms, for example) and science (where a Grand Unified Theory of physics is an ongoing project amongst the community), is also investigated. The turn against universal theories in philosophy in recent decades (as in the case of Marxism), is considered in the concluding section.

Keywords Universal theories • Bad faith • Marxism • Monotheism • Conspiracy theory • Existentialism • Jean-Paul Sartre • Denialism • Science

Universal theories continue to have a detrimental effect on geopolitics, all too often substituting faith for reason—bad faith in most cases, as sceptics would definitely want to contend—and being highly resistant to

© The Author(s), under exclusive license to Springer Nature Switzerland AG 2025
S. Sim, *Sartre, Existentialism, and the New Age of Nausea*, https://doi.org/10.1007/978-3-031-90774-6_4

alternative explanations and viewpoints. Dogmatism comes to dominate thinking instead, and that is never a good trait to find in a democracy; in effect, the antithesis of the temperament that is required if political discourse is going to work for the benefit of all. Marxism was a classic instance of this tendency in its refusal to acknowledge the validity of other political theories or philosophies, arguing that it was the only true universal theory, a 'science of society' which could not be bettered as its thinkers saw it, and all too willing to use violence to impose it on others: a policy which was to have a profound effect on world politics. Bad faith in unapologetic action one might be inclined to say in retrospect, although there is no denying that it attracted many followers worldwide until that side of it became too obvious to ignore. Monotheistic religions are guilty of the same kind of hostile attitude towards diversity, hence the many, extremely violent and unforgiving, 'wars of religion' that punctuate modern history and are still there in the background of geopolitics (in the Middle East and India notably enough, but they have the potential to break out anywhere religious fundamentalism thrives).

Existentialism is opposed to universal theories in general, although that created difficulties for Sartre in a period when left-wing politics was strongly influenced by Marxism and the Communist Party was a very powerful force in France. *What Is Literature?*, written in the immediate post-war period, reveals just how critical he could be of the Party's motives and aims. Sartre eventually attempted to reconcile the two theories in his *Critique of Dialectical Reason*, but not all that successfully. For all his determined, and no doubt sincere, efforts, that was never likely to be a completely viable project. The theories are designed to do very different, basically incompatible, things and in consequence clash in too many fundamental aspects for followers of either side to be comfortable with any projected synthesis. Marxism assumes a pattern in history developing in a predictable, determinate manner; a dialectic working through every living being towards a clearly defined end. For Sartre, however, this was little more than a misguided attempt 'to control human history from outside' which in effect denied the freedom of individual human beings, one of the central tenets of his philosophy.[1] He insisted instead that 'it is not the dialectic which forces historical men to live their history in terrible contradictions; it is men, as they are, dominated by scarcity and necessity'.[2] The notion of forces within nature determining human outcomes does not fit with an existentialist worldview, which emphasises our freedom to choose our own course of action throughout life, even if it has to be accepted that things like scarcity and necessity might conspire to limit our scope.

Existentialism certainly fits in with left-wing politics in a general sense, as Sartre himself did throughout his career; but Marxism poses more problems for it, both philosophically and ideologically, than, say, just socialism does. Authenticity, as a case in point, is hard to maintain in a system structured on following the party line unquestioningly. Can one really be authentic following directions as to what you should think and do that eventually can be traced back to a decision made by a strong leader? (or at best, a central committee). As Sarah Bakewell has summed it up: 'The Party demanded the kind of commitment that means never having to think again': uncritical belief, in other words, which is never going to mesh with an existentialist worldview.[3] (At the other end of the political spectrum, William Irwin's book *The Free Market Existentialist* has tried to claim existentialism for both capitalism and political libertarianism.[4] Yet for all Sartre's critical stance towards communism, that seems more than a bit of a leap to make—not one I would care to endorse anyway.)

The trend in philosophy since existentialism has been very much antiuniversal theory, as in the case of poststructuralism and postmodernism, where thinkers like Jean-François Lyotard and Michel Foucault have taken a very sceptical line against this tradition. For Foucault, Marxism was a product of nineteenth-century culture that had now lost its relevance: 'Marxism exists in nineteenth-century thought like a fish in water: that is, it is unable to breathe anywhere else'.[5] So much for a science of society holding over time (Foucault was similarly critical of Sartre's *Critique of Dialectical Reason*, seeing it as too rooted in nineteenth-century thought to be applicable to contemporary social and political concerns). Lyotard's *Libidinal Economy* goes on to reject Marx's work in even stronger terms, arguing that '[w]e must come to take Marx as if he were a writer, an author full of affects, take his text as a madness and not as a theory'.[6] Predictably, that assessment did not go down well with the Marxist community, for which *The Communist Manifesto* was no mere narrative but the definitive handbook on how to resolve the world's social and political problems, with *Capital* going on to provide all the theoretical background that could ever be needed to justify the project.[7] As with Sartre's critique of communism (discussed in more detail below), this only served to alienate Lyotard from his erstwhile left-wing colleagues, further proof of the inability to accept dissent within the territory of universal theory.

Conspiracy theory operates in a similar manner to universal theories in claiming to be the only correct explanation of whatever phenomenon it is focused on, in that both rely heavily on the uncritical belief of adherents, which is to be kept free of doubt or scrutiny and resistant to compromise. Critical analysis has no part to play in the enterprise. And since conspiracies can be generated by just about anything if you put your mind to it (we are awash with them at present, as any check of social media will soon reveal), there is never any lack of opportunities available for the multitude of uncritical believers out there to sign themselves up for. (Once out there, as well, they stay there indefinitely. Old conspiracy theories never die: one only has to look around on social media to find the old favourites, such as faked moon landings and 9/11, still lurking.) If belief is the problem with bad faith, then uncritical belief is its most developed, and most resistant, strain. Yet again, denialism plays a large part in the process, keeping adversary viewpoints at a distance; conspiracists being notably quick to present a united front to their critics. Bad faith is much in evidence here, as in the concepts of 'fake news' and 'alternative facts', which, conveniently enough, can always be found by the committed to prove their point and disprove yours—conclusively, as they see it. Arguments for authenticity are particularly needed to counter this dangerous drift into post-truth, which is becoming a hallmark of the far-right mentality. There is a cult-like character to note about such thinking, where preservation of the theory and its doctrines takes precedence over everything else and will be defended to the hilt by the faithful. The rule would appear to be: if in doubt, deny, and then go on denying as long as you are challenged. Diversity of opinion is manifestly unwelcome in such circles.

The search for a 'theory of everything' permeates all areas of human endeavour, from the religious through the political to the scientific. In the case of the latter, there is a willingness to keep altering the theory to fit new data as it is discovered in experiments—and these days there is a wealth of this, coming on stream constantly. When it comes to the religious, however, such an approach tends to be viewed as heretical and dogma prevails, as zealously guarded by the priesthood in each case (if one were to be cynical about it they might be described as defenders of the bad faith, and they can always be found as well). The political can be just as resistant when it chooses to be, as the history of communism clearly illustrates; the principle there being that the dialectic must be maintained at all costs as a scientific fact, otherwise the party's authority might begin to slip away (hence the various highly spurious attempts, from Friedrich Engels onwards, to establish the dialectic as a fundamental law of nature[8]). Universal theories in general are not open to reform when it comes to their basics, nor much given to reflection as to their justification. As Hannah Arendt has observed in her study of totalitarianism: 'the last century has produced an abundance of ideologies that pretend to be keys to history but are actually nothing but desperate attempts to escape responsibility'.[9] That neatly summarises bad faith in the realm of sciences of society in general.

SARTRE VERSUS COMMUNISM

Sartre's scepticism regarding communism comes to the fore in *What Is Literature?*, which is notably scathing about its methods, arguing that Communist writing, as a case in point, 'places itself above all debate' and thus is not to be trusted.[10] As has been noted at several points in the book so far, this is a typical assumption of universal theories, which invariably consider themselves to have a foolproof system of belief, thus to be in possession of the answers to everything. Criticism is never welcomed, or even much heeded. Marxism again constitutes a classic case study of the process. For Sartre that meant '[t]he politics of Stalinist Communism is incompatible in France with the honest practice of the literary craft'.[11] Communism never did encourage, or even much tolerate, debate, especially after it came to power; to question the party line was viewed as close to treason in such circumstances and punished accordingly. Russia provided many grisly examples of how far the party was prepared to go to ensure compliance with its dictates, with various famous writers and artists being imprisoned or liquidated for holding unorthodox views (which could include refusing to adopt the socialist realism style the party insisted upon throughout the arts, a style which has not weathered well at all). For Sartre, however, such questioning was absolutely integral to writing, thus censorship (including self-censorship, which universal theories tend to invoke in believers as a safety procedure) was to be rejected. The whole point of writing was to challenge convention, not to endorse it, to provoke debate not close it down; when that does not happen then authoritarianism simply grows stronger and opposition and dissent all the harder to express. Existentialism always has to conceive of itself as in opposition to that state of affairs, always at the very least sceptical of universal theories, where bad faith is too much in evidence. No theory, existentialism included, can consider itself to be beyond debate—even if that means having to defend itself against being unintentionally pro-capitalist and libertarian in intent. That sort of exchange is precisely what theorists, open-minded ones anyway, ought to relish involvement in.

Religion as Universal Theory

Monotheistic religions assume that they apply universally, and traditionally have refused to recognise the claims of their competitors, arguing that they supersede all existing belief systems. Their god made the universe and their god controls what happens in it, right down to the very last detail, being the unwavering party line, and once they are powerful enough to do so this will become the rule for everyone they come into contact with, who will be expected to submit to it. Thus the drive to Christianize the globe during the days of Western colonial expansion, to recast it as their religion dictated it should be, in obedience to the will of their god alone. All other religions were simply misguided. Religious wars have been the natural consequence of this unconciliatory mind-set, demonstrating the extent to which monotheisms believe they are beyond any debate at all. The 'mono' is to be taken seriously, and this can even create problems within the one religion: as with Catholics and Protestants in the Christian tradition, and Sunni and Shia in the Islamic. Such divisions have to raise some awkward questions about where ultimate authority lies, enough to start the odd sectarian war over the years, and can still be a source of tension in places like Northern Ireland. Even if the major religions now, grudgingly or otherwise, at least tolerate each other's existence (plus factions within their own), none of them concedes that this invalidates their own claims to universality and being the only really true belief about the nature of things. They do not see themselves as mere narratives in that respect, as anyone outside their own particular system will be inclined to, but as the one and only truth that all should adhere to without exception.

Monotheism offers a way of explaining everything that happens in human history, putting it down to some version or other of 'God's will' (your own god being the only true one of course). In other words, there is an underlying order and plan to the universe and human existence within that, as a careful reading of one's holy book—the Bible, or Koran, etc.—will reveal. There are no loose ends in that respect, nothing contingent—as existentialism insists being is, something we are 'thrown' into (as Martin Heidegger had argued in *Being and Time*[12]) and have to negotiate from there without any master plan to guide us. In a monotheistic framework everything fits together seamlessly; very much a case of human history being controlled from outside. Even in an age when, in the West at least, secularism is widespread in public life, such ideas still exert considerable influence. Politicians have to tread warily around questions of religion, for example, for fear of alienating believers amongst the electorate, as they definitely have to in America, where such matters are taken far more seriously than they are in Western Europe these days. One suspects bad faith just has to be occurring in some cases, but in public all candidates for high political office in the USA have to profess to being religious: Christian preferably, as the socially and politically very influential religious right movement there is (to date there has been no non-Christian president). Hence the belief amongst Republican voters that the assassination attempt on Donald Trump during the presidential campaign in 2024 was unsuccessful because of divine intervention. 'I had God on my side', as Trump told the subsequent Republican convention, which took his claim quite literally—all to the benefit of his campaign and, one has to assume, to his subsequent re-election. And as far as the American religious right was concerned, that could only be the Christian god (given the evangelical bias to this movement, one would feel inclined to say the Protestant Christian god as well). Belief here is total and unconditional, uncritical to a fault, America's multiculturalism notwithstanding. (Whether God is also responsible for the torrent of disinformation about elections in America, and elsewhere, to be found on social media is another issue again; but then, as the faithful keep telling us, God moves in mysterious ways that mere humanity can never hope to fathom. More mysterious ways might be spotted perhaps in the Russian Orthodox Church's support of Vladimir Putin and his invasion of Ukraine.)

Monotheistic religion with its promise of an afterlife could be seen as an attempt to overcome the threat of nothingness, and its popularity over the last few millennia would be understandable on those grounds alone. Nothingness is hardly a comforting prospect psychologically speaking, nor is absurdity, and theories to the contrary will find a ready audience in that regard—as religions have long since realised and capitalised on. Pascal's wager can always be brought in to provide an intellectual backup to religion's essentially emotional appeal, on the grounds that you have much to gain from believing in god if there is one, but nothing to lose if there turns out not to be. One can appreciate why some would choose him as a fellow-traveller on that basis. For the secular, however, there can be no such reprieve, and to take refuge either in belief in the afterlife or in the wager can only qualify as being unauthentic. It is not an issue we can pretend does not exist, as Roquentin's nausea keeps reminding him. If there really is nothing out there, then how do we make sense of, or justify, our actions? Or even our continued existence, as Albert Camus so dramatically poses the problem in *The Myth of Sisyphus*: 'There is but one truly serious philosophical problem and that is suicide. Judging whether life is or is not worth living amounts to answering the fundamental question of philosophy'.[13] Neither is it just philosophers who have such psychologically disturbing thoughts, they can assail any of us at any time.

Although it faces an uphill task against monotheism, liberal democratic humanism can be brought in as a substitute for religion, and universal theories in general. It is not a set belief but rather a range of ideals and aspirations that can change over time, and that has to be one of its main selling points for the sceptically oriented thinker (John Gray, as we shall see in the next chapter, would vehemently disagree however). It can mean various things to various people, therefore, but at least it is clear about what it does not believe in: authoritarianism in any of its guises, and the bad faith which invariably underpins this system to our general detriment. Liberal humanism has no need of strong leaders, and that has to be seen as one of its major virtues. It is a system which at its best runs from the bottom up (the electorate), rather than the top down, making it much more responsive to social and political change.

SCIENCE AND THE SEARCH FOR A GRAND UNIFIED THEORY

Although it has not always done so in the past, when its own version of denialism could often be seen in operation amongst its establishment (often hand in hand with the religious authorities, unsurprisingly enough, as in the infamous case of Galileo), science now allows debate over its theories and is open to revising these on the basis of new findings. That is, as long as those findings have been rigorously researched and tested: evidence still counts in the scientific world, which is not always the case in either political authoritarianism or religion. An assumption of provisionality is wired into the scientific enterprise nowadays, and in areas such as physics this means that changes have been coming thick and fast—much to the bewilderment of any lay-person trying to keep up (especially in notoriously complex areas such as quantum mechanics, which stretch rationality and credibility more than somewhat, for scientists as well as the general public). Nevertheless, science is just as concerned to be a theory of everything; hence the obsession with constructing a 'Grand Unified Theory' (GUT) in physics. There is a so-called standard model in this area which physicists have been working systematically to complete, with many claiming that they are tantalisingly close to doing so. Although it works well in general, there are still significant gaps in it that are proving very difficult indeed to resolve. Dark matter and dark energy, for example, remain highly elusive entities, being neither fully understood nor explained, despite intense speculation over many years as to their exact nature (and since combined they make up c. 95% of the universe according to the standard model, this is a major issue). Some scientists have even suggested that, given the many anomalies associated with it, the standard model itself is no longer fit for purpose, but for the time being it continues to be the main point of reference in physics, although it is always to be treated as open to modification. (One interesting recent idea is that the model is based on false premises, of being able to posit an objective perspective to understand reality from, thereby ignoring the crucial human element inescapably involved in any scientific enterprise. We have a 'blind spot' about this, which scientists ought to be taking account of in their researches.[14] The phenomenological bias displayed here ought to be appreciated by existentialists.)

Whether a GUT will ever be reached is an interesting metaphysical question; there may always be something missing from it, as there currently is, thus casting doubt on the whole notion of a 'universal' theory. That is the implication of the work of theorists like John D. Barrow, who argued in his book *Impossibility*, that there are limits to what we can know or even find answers to, a situation no less true now than when he was making those points more than twenty years ago. For the scientific world it may seem to be the case that a theory of everything is finally coming together, '[b]ut then something unexpected happens' and yet further work is required to explain what has caused this.[15] So far this has been the recurrent pattern. Nevertheless, it is a question that scientists are at least willing to debate, and science as an activity is not as such dependent on the answer; as Barrow observes, it will continue on as before, creating as comprehensive a model of the physical universe as it is able to from its experiments, and incorporating new findings from there as best it can. Existing theories will be revised, tweaked or replaced as necessary, while maintaining the discipline's principles.

Religions, however, never can be willing to go anything like that far. Their standard model is not to be tinkered with in any way, it reached completion a long time ago as far as its theorists are concerned, and its authority is heavily dependent on the weight of history that lies behind that. (Creationism gives us a particularly literal-minded version of this tendency as regards the Christian standard model. Based on its reading of the model's foundation, the Bible, it reduces the Earth's age to the span of the generations listed there plus those since Jesus' lifetime, coming up with a figure somewhere around the 10,000-year mark. A streamlined theory of everything one might say, if one needing a large dose of bad faith on the part of adherents to make it work.) The same goes for fundamentalist-inclined ideological systems such as Marxism or fascism, whose reflex reaction will always be to reject all evidence to the contrary and to do whatever they can to suppress it; again, they are quite satisfied with their own standard model and see no reason to doubt its validity or universal application. Questioning their assumptions is never going to be acceptable to their leaders, whose power derives from these and the tradition, plus its key figures of authority, that they spring from. You can no more take issue with Marx or Engels than you can with the Christian god or Allah; to do so is to offer yourself up as a target for true believers, who are always on the lookout for heretics. Tradition dies very hard in such discourses, and blind spots linger on, unhelpfully so (politically as well as philosophically). Taking authority as sacrosanct is never going to be a good policy, either in politics or religion. Science has a far healthier attitude towards those in power, a greater willingness to challenge the status quo (even the greatest scientists throughout history can find their theories being disproved eventually). Ideally, this is the way all universal theories should operate, but along with monotheistic religions most political theories fail that test also, as the next prominent example will demonstrate.

Philosophy as Anti-Universal Theory

As noted above, there has been a distinct turn against universal theory in the philosophical world in the wake of Marxism's decline in the political realm. Post-Marxism, for example, has completely distanced itself from this side of the Marxist tradition, casting real doubt on the theory's overall value, in what could be described as a calculated act of 'self-recovery'. As the major theorists of the movement, Ernesto Laclau and Chantal Mouffe, so bluntly put it, '[t]he "evident truths" of the past' on which left-wing thought for so long had been based, 'have been seriously challenged by an avalanche of historical mutations which have riven the ground on which those truths were constituted'.[16] Marxist true believers did not agree with this sweeping claim and made their disapproval only too plain in what became a particularly acrimonious dispute that ran on for several years in left-wing circles. To the latter the evident truths still held; to post-Marxists that was the equivalent of being in bad faith and stubbornly refusing to recognise that the reason your theory was not working as predicted was because it had serious flaws. That is a problem all universal theories eventually are faced by, however; that theory and reality inevitably will diverge at some point, to the detriment of the former's credibility. No standard model can be considered timeless. The Soviet system was to collapse just a few years after Laclau and Mouffe's intervention on the theoretical front, as if to underline the point that such divergence cannot be disguised forever, that 'awakening' is always a possibility in even the least promising of contexts (as most outsiders would have defined the Soviet system as being). Marxism's importance as both philosophy and political theory has been in sharp decline ever since. Plainly, something unexpected did happen, and the theory was not prepared for this eventuality. It still has its believers, but they are a dwindling band with diminishing influence on the wider scene.

Even before the emergence of post-Marxism as a specific theory in its own right, questions had been raised about Marxism's authoritarian bias by some of its influential supporters. Despite being a highly respected Marxist theorist of long standing, Theodor W. Adorno was to argue that there was an identifiably totalitarian cast to Marxist thought which meant it was unwilling to countenance opposition, especially from within its own ranks, from where uncritical belief was expected (and enforced, often quite ruthlessly). Adorno was dismissive of the very notion of a totalising, universally applicable, philosophy such as Marxism's 'science of society' claimed to be, asserting emphatically that 'a total philosophy is no longer to be hoped for'.[17] Since then both poststructuralist and postmodernist philosophers have been resolutely anti-totalising in their approach, seeing existence as being far more random and unpredictable than Marxists take it to be (with Michel Foucault and Jean-François Lyotard in the vanguard of this movement). In common with Sartre, they reject determinisms of any kind. Nevertheless, when it comes to the realm of politics, universal theory continues to exert considerable appeal amongst the general public, especially when it is allied to conspiracy theory and its ready-made audience in the social media community, who refuse even to consider the possibility of blind spots on their behalf. As with the Marxist establishment, ranks close on this issue and meaningful debate tends to be shut down. It is no surprise that the far right is able to capitalise on this tendency, as it leans unmistakably towards autocracy.

Again, we find ourselves being treated to a quest narrative, Marxism basing itself on a supposed dialectic working its way through history, expressing itself in the form of class struggle, with a different social group rising to dominance in each age, having overcome the previously most powerful: a movement from thesis to antithesis to synthesis, in the model formulated by Marx's main philosophical influence G. W. F. Hegel in *The Philosophy of History*.[18] The quest will lead eventually to an end to class struggle, making way for the 'dictatorship of the proletariat'; in effect, an end to the economic exploitation of the mass of humanity by the corporate world of capitalism. It was a powerful narrative and it underpinned communism as it established itself in Europe in the aftermath of World War I, having a profound impact on world politics for much of the twentieth century (especially when it spread to China as well after World War II). It was billed by Marxism as a 'science of society' rooted in human development over time, but there is no scientific proof that such a dialectic ever actually existed or could be turned to account as Marxism had envisaged, with revolutions (such as in Russia in 1917) serving to accelerate the process, according to the theory. It is all rather too neat as an explanation of human history, which, as poststructuralists have argued, is far more random and unpredictable than Marxists would have us believe. 'Events', as Lyotard pictures it, just keep disrupting any plan to impose an overall pattern onto history; an event being, 'the impact, on the system, of floods of energy such that the system does not manage to bind and channel this energy'.[19] History is a series of these, rather than a steady progression to the predetermined end that Marxism posits; the unexpected continually gets in the way instead, as the volatile state of world politics at present only too obviously goes to show. Adorno's point was that even if a dialectic did exist, then it would just continue to unfold, thesis generating new antithesis over and over again, rather than to resolve itself in the manner that Marxism required, heading towards an ultimate synthesis as Hegel had postulated.

If there is no dialectic as proposed then Marxism turns into just another fictional narrative, and narratives can always be contested (and in a democratic society must be if autocracy is to be kept at bay). It becomes yet another candidate for aesthetic judgement, as do most religions for the secularly inclined. We can understand why they would appeal—universal explanations always do, by making life at least seem easier to understand, right down to the level of the individual—but that does not make them true, or even defensible after a certain point. Fiction does not lend itself to such analysis, it is either interesting or not, thought-provoking or not, but questions of truth-value do not, and can not, arise. Neither do 'events' have to be watched out for, as they manifestly do in the invented narratives of conspiracy or far-right theorists with their deliberately unacknowledged blind spots. That the far right can always find an appropriate 'event' to justify their actions, however violent and anti-social these may be, should be enough on its own to make us suspicious of their narratives and what they are trying to achieve through them. It is always valid, and necessary, to ask who gains from this narrative, and why? Furthermore, why does it require uncritical belief on our part? Whatever does insist on that has to be viewed with suspicion, as it most likely signals that we are being manipulated by someone seeking power over us.

Notes

1. Jean-Paul Sartre, *Critique of Dialectical Reason* (1960), trans. Alan Sheridan-Smith, London and New York: Verso, 1991, p. 34.
2. Ibid., p. 37.
3. Sarah Bakewell, *At the Existentialist Cafe: Freedom, Being and Apricot Cocktails*, London: Vintage, 2017, p. 252.
4. See William Irwin, *The Free Market Existentialist: Capitalism Without Consumerism*, Hoboken, NJ: Wiley, 2015.
5. Michel Foucault, *The Order of Things: An Archaeology of the Human Sciences* (1966), trans. Alan Sheridan-Smith, London: Tavistock, 1970, p. 262.
6. Jean-François Lyotard, *Libidinal Economy* (1974), trans. Iain Hamilton Grant, London: Athlone Press, 1993, p. 95.
7. Karl Marx and Friedrich Engels, *The Communist Manifesto* (1848), ed. Frederic L. Bender, New York and London: W. W. Norton, 1988; Karl Marx, *Capital*, I–IV (1867, 1885, 1894, 1905–10), London: Lawrence and Wishart, 1978.

8. See, for example, Friedrich Engels, *Anti-Dühring: Herr Eugen Dühring's Revolution in Science* (1878), Peking: Foreign Language Press, 1976.
9. Hannah Arendt, *The Origins of Totalitarianism* (1951), London: Penguin, 2017, pp. 10–11.
10. Jean-Paul Sartre, *What Is Literature?* (1948), trans. Bernard Frechtman, London: Methuen, 1967, p. 190.
11. Ibid., p. 189.
12. Martin Heidegger, *Being and Time*, trans. John Macquarrie and Edward Robinson, Oxford: Basil Blackwell, 1980.
13. Albert Camus, *The Myth of Sisyphus*, (1942), trans. Justin O'Brien, Harmondsworth: Penguin, 1975, p. 11.
14. See Adam Frank, et al., *The Blind Spot: Why Science Cannot Ignore Human Experience*, Cambridge, MA: MIT Press, 2024.
15. John D. Barrow, *Impossibility: The Limits of Science and the Science of Limits*, London: Vintage, 1999, p. 249.
16. Ernesto Laclau and Chantal Mouffe, *Hegemony and Socialist Strategy: Towards a Radical Democratic Politics*, London: Verso, 1985, p. 1.
17. Theodor W. Adorno, *Negative Dialectics*, trans. E. B. Ashton, London: Routledge and Kegan Paul, 1973, p. 136.
18. See G. W. F. Hegel, *The Philosophy of History*, trans. J. Sibree, New York: Dover, 1956.
19. Jean-François Lyotard, *Political Writings*, trans. Bill Readings and Kevin Paul Geiman, London: UCL Press, 1993, p. 64.

References

Adorno, Theodor W., *Negative Dialectics*, trans. E. B. Ashton, London: Routledge and Kegan Paul, 1973.

Bakewell, Sarah, *At the Existentialist Cafe: Freedom, Being and Apricot Cocktails*, London: Vintage, 2017.

Barrow, John D., *Impossibility: The Limits of Science and the Science of Limits*, London: Vintage, 1999.

Camus, Albert, *The Myth of Sisyphus*, (1942), trans. Justin O'Brien, Harmondsworth: Penguin, 1975.

Engels, Friedrich, *Anti-Dühring: Herr Eugen Dühring's Revolution in Science* (1878), Peking: Foreign Language Press, 1976.

Foucault, Michel, *The Order of Things: An Archaeology of the Human Sciences* (1966), trans. Alan Sheridan-Smith, London: Tavistock, 1970.

Frank, Adam, et al., *The Blind Spot: Why Science Cannot Ignore Human Experience*, Cambridge, MA: MIT Press, 2024.

Hegel, G. W. F., *The Philosophy of History*, trans. J. Sibree, New York: Dover, 1956.

Heidegger, Martin, *Being and Time*, trans. John Macquarrie and Edward Robinson, Oxford: Basil Blackwell, 1980.

Irwin, William, *The Free Market Existentialist: Capitalism Without Consumerism*, Hoboken, NJ: Wiley, 2015.

Laclau, Ernesto and Chantal Mouffe, *Hegemony and Socialist Strategy: Towards a Radical Democratic Politics*, London: Verso, 1985.

Lyotard, Jean-François, *Libidinal Economy* (1974), trans. Iain Hamilton Grant, London: Athlone Press, 1993.

———. *Political Writings*, trans. Bill Readings and Kevin Paul Geiman, London: UCL Press, 1993.

Marx, Karl, *Capital*, I–IV (1867, 1885, 1894, 1905–10), London: Lawrence and Wishart, 1978.

———. and Friedrich Engels, *The Communist Manifesto* (1848), ed. Frederic L. Bender, New York and London: W. W. Norton, 1988.

Sartre, Jean-Paul, *Nausea* (1938), trans. Robert Baldick, Harmondsworth: Penguin, 1965.

———. *What Is Literature?* (1948), trans. Bernard Frechtman, London: Methuen, 1967.

———. *Critique of Dialectical Reason* (1960), trans. Alan Sheridan-Smith, London and New York: Verso, 1991.

CHAPTER 5

A Somewhat Despairing Conclusion on Human Weakness

Abstract This concluding chapter adopts a rather despairing attitude to our current socio-political situation, and how we have collectively allowed it to develop to a point where it so closely resembles the chaotic state of the late 1930s. Democracy is clearly under threat when authoritarianism is so very much in the ascendancy, exploiting the many flashpoints that the geopolitical landscape is constantly generating. A 'positive pessimism' is advocated in response, taking a more realistic, existentialism-influenced, attitude to our plight and how to cope with it in the face of adversity. The far more negatively oriented pessimism found in John Gray's recent book *The New Leviathans* is critiqued and held to be seriously wanting as an analysis of the international political scene. The value of existentialism in making sense of a world where authoritarians, climate change sceptics and conspiracists are creating such a toxic atmosphere in public life is re-emphasised.

Keywords Denialism • Jean-Paul Sartre • *Nausea* • Bad faith • Democracy • Authoritarianism • Democracy • Authenticity • John Gray

If nothing else, the popularity of the 'politics of prejudice' and the anti-woke movement it has spawned, as well as the voluble ranks of climate sceptics and their assumption of being 'above all debate', denialists to the

© The Author(s), under exclusive license to Springer Nature Switzerland AG 2025
S. Sim, *Sartre, Existentialism, and the New Age of Nausea*, https://doi.org/10.1007/978-3-031-90774-6_5

end, signal that we are collectively capable of repeating the mistakes of the 1930s and 40s. We could even be said to be on the verge of doing so, with flashpoints continually cropping up in what is proving to be an increasingly volatile geopolitical landscape full of unexpected twists and turns. While there are always tensions in that respect, generally they can be more or less contained through pragmatic diplomatic activity and the overall system kept functioning reasonably efficiently. Bearing in mind chaos theory, however, sometimes the system breaks down altogether, having gone past a critical tipping point. Every major war that occurs is evidence that humanity is very prone to creating just such conditions and then struggling to deal with the aftermath of failing to reach a compromise in time. The situation now is eerily similar to what it was when Sartre was writing *Nausea* and just such a tipping point was looming ominously in the sociopolitical order. There has been a definite shift to the right internationally, ideologically speaking, that is alarming in its implications to anyone of a democratic disposition. It is noticeable that fears of World War III are being openly voiced by political commentators more and more frequently of late, and looking around at the current state of affairs politically and the many intractable differends it is bringing to light, as well as glaring examples of bad faith, it is not hard to see why. The Middle East has been unstable for years and is even more so now; it would not take much for that to trigger a major war, inexorably drawing in the world's major powers such as America and Russia (and quite possibly China too). That is, to say the least, a frightening prospect, but it is one that we cannot discount with the shake-up of the world order that the second Trump presidency is highly likely to cause (indeed, seeks to cause in the name of MAGA). It is a state of affairs which can change dramatically from day to day, not always with much warning; as in the closing stages of *The Reprieve*, no-one really knows what will come next.[1]

Just to increase one's sense of despair, there are also fears of civil war (or at the very least, large-scale civil disorder that could become very violent) breaking out in countries like America, and even the UK, as the far right asserts itself ever more aggressively on the political stage. The project therefore concludes with some admittedly rather pessimistic reflections on human behaviour and the continued appeal of authoritarian, antidemocratic ideologies such as fascism. The value of an existentialist outlook in facing up to such challenges will be re-emphasised (particularly the critical role that authenticity has to play), as will the need to keep countering them no matter how powerful they may become. Neither authoritarianism nor climate change is going to go away, they require our constant attention; especially since the former is one of the main barriers to positive action being taken on the latter, which has to rank as one of the worst examples of bad faith in a world that is currently full of them. The greater public good is never going to be a concern of the authoritarian temperament, which cannot be trusted at all to protect the environment, or listen to calls from the rest of the population to act that way. Authoritarians are not open to suggestion from those they want to exert control over.

The bias may be pessimistic therefore, but as set out in the introductory chapter I will be arguing from the point of view of a 'positive' pessimism, as opposed to that put forward recently by John Gray in *The New Leviathans: Thoughts After Liberalism* (a work which will be engaged with in more detail below).[2] That is, a pessimism that faces up to reality as it is and refuses to let it depress one to the extent of giving up trying to rectify the situation as much as one can: a response I would take to be in line with the existentialist cause. We should always be seeking out the authentic way to confront events, no matter how unpleasant and apparently insoluble they may appear to be. There is no point in denying that nausea could descend on us at any moment in such situations, incapacitating our ability to act normally. By making us intensely aware of the precariousness of our existence that is what crisis can do, and it is crisis more than anything that seems to underpin the current standard model of politics, where worst-case scenarios are entirely possible outcomes to be borne in mind all the time. That was the case in the late 1930s and it is again now. It also looks set to be for the foreseeable future. Small wonder then that so many opt to hide that uncomfortable truth from themselves, as they do also with the dire projections associated with climate crisis, which can amplify our experience of precariousness to a yet more extreme level: the late 1930s plus plus. Neither is the thought of settling Mars likely to improve our state of mind by much.

Nevertheless, like Roquentin we have to learn to move on from that state, no matter how often it may happen or how debilitating it may feel; being authentic demands no less, whether or not yet another World War looms menacingly on the horizon. There are, as Sartre insists, always choices to be made even in the darkest of times and most desperate of conditions. He gives a particularly provocative example of this in *Being and Nothingness*, when he argues that 'even torture does not dispossess us of our freedom; when we give in, we do so freely'.[3] The implication is that if we do give in and release the information the torturers want, then we have in effect decided to collaborate with them. It is a claim that has been heavily criticised, with one commentator complaining 'this seems to fly in the face of reality', and it does seem to be pushing the notion of freedom further than is reasonable—certainly, further than most commentators feel able to defend without some more stretching and bending of Sartre's concepts.[4] What Sartre is determined to show, however, is that there is always an authentic line to be identified and followed if we are prepared to brave it. If we can excuse the melodrama of that example (this was after all written in times of war when dreadful things were happening all around, torture notably included on the fascist side), that is still a point worth making. (Few of us would blame anyone who could not summon up such courage under those circumstances anyway; doing one's best not to collaborate for as long as one could manage would be acceptable to most.) The dividing line between the keen awareness of authenticity that Sartre expects individuals to feel and authoritarianism remains quite clear: good faith versus bad faith is a choice that is open to any of us, no matter how restricted it may be by outside events. That is what constitutes our freedom as Sartre sees it, and it is something that we have to keep thinking about, because bad faith can catch us out at any point in our dealings with others. Authenticity means having to make choices all the time.

The Return of Fascism

One would have thought that after the well-documented horrors of World War II fascism would no longer hold any appeal, except to the most extreme of temperaments. Yet it has returned to the political scene in various European countries, and support for it has been growing steadily in recent years. Why that should be so, given what we know happened only a few generations ago and is still a vivid part of folk memory, has to be a mystery to most of us, but its ability to keep working its way back into the political system, regardless of how much liberal opposition is organised against it, has to be acknowledged. That has to be a significant source of worry, leaving us to wonder just how safe the concept of liberal democracy actually is, how resilient to hostile outside forces. Fascism has drawn many studies from the time of World War II onwards and has been carefully and systematically analysed in terms of the psychology it involves (Hannah Arendt being a prominent contributor to this literature[5]), but despite that it never quite seems to go away, nor that psychology from re-emerging.

Neither is it just a fringe phenomenon of little real import. Instead, it is attracting support from across the political spectrum and is now effectively part of the mainstream in European politics, a development very few would have thought likely even just a short while ago. One has to assume as well that no-one can fail to know something about fascism's sordid past; yet somehow or other a significant number of our fellow citizens feel able to ignore that, to have decided instead that fascism can offer a solution to our political ills (as they conceive of them anyway), and that strong leaders represent our salvation from these. Or perhaps to have 'forgotten' this episode in our history, as Jean-François Lyotard claimed figures like Martin Heidegger had, in the aftermath of World War II.[6] By which Lyotard meant, far more judgementally, had conveniently 'chosen to' forget in order to make their lives easier in the changed political circumstances they found themselves having to negotiate: false fellow-travellers in that regard. Neither explanation is exactly easy to live with, but the fact is that fascism is now back in open circulation and thus part of our daily lives; a situation that will need exceedingly careful monitoring by democrats everywhere.

There is also a substantial cohort of 'Holocaust deniers' to contend with, part of the ever-expanding conspiracy theory movement that is turning into one of the great growth industries of contemporary culture. The persistence of denialism is one of the most depressing features of our time: surely a case of the absurd at its most absurd, a trait that cannot be defended on any grounds. Reflecting on such issues it is hard not to think of the end of rationality, of an encounter with Sartre's nothingness, or of Immanuel Kant's sublime; the point at which theories of everything fail, the nausea moment when nothing seems to make sense any more and we are at a complete loss as to what to do.[7] It is what science is wrestling with when it comes to black holes, where, as a *New Scientist* feature somewhat apocalyptically puts it, 'space-time ends' as 'physics breaks down'.[8] And then to wonder whether we have to consider if something similar lurks within human psychology. Scapegoating would appear to be one of its telltale signs: Jews in the 1930s, immigrants now, some vulnerable group can always be found by those whose narrative needs it, logic playing no part in the choice. Bad faith is dictating the state of play at such junctures, deliberately closing itself off from all other points of view, as if the scapegoated group had no right to existence at all. Fascism constitutes a black hole as far as democratic principles go, the point at which rationality breaks down and debate is eradicated from the political process, to be replaced by the threat of violence if you do not conform to the ruling elite's dictates. You are not going to be allowed to debate with a strong leader in a one-party state; even being critical of one such from outside the state itself can put your life at risk, as many dissidents have found to their cost in recent years: 'transnational repression' as it has been described.[9]

The strong leader doctrine really needs to be confronted and critiqued constantly, because it is so engrained in our culture that it all too easily becomes a reflex response to political or social crises. It has to be one of humanity's greatest weaknesses that we give in to this so often, proof that power attracts—and to paraphrase the old saying a bit further, perhaps it could be added that absolute power attracts absolutely, which is not a particularly comforting thought for anyone of a liberal outlook to have to ponder. Nor is the doctrine ever a good solution to crisis, regardless of how much support it might drum up, because it tends to gravitate, and usually quite rapidly, to totalitarianism. Politically, it is a recurrent feature of the last century or so, with examples running from Mussolini and Hitler through to Donald Trump and Vladimir Putin (note how it is male figures who dominate in any such list, where bullying is a major part of the political style).

Taking an even longer perspective, the notion of a messiah figure regularly appears in monotheisms, with that figure invariably being described as a saviour for all of humanity (a male saviour again, characteristically). Not just the saviour but the only possible saviour as well, brooking no debate on that matter, uncritical belief being demanded right from the start. Monotheisms have long depended on eliciting a positive reaction from the public at large to this claim (the messiah complex, as it were), and its success over the centuries is evidence of the significant hold it has over the popular imagination—a hold that needs to be resisted when it spreads into so many other areas of our culture. Authoritarianism exploits this aspect of human nature, and does so with ruthless efficiency: to the point of abolishing opposition and elections if necessary to ensure the assumed saviour's domination. Absolute power for ever is the motivating goal, with no restraining checks or balances to get in the way of wielding this over the masses. Frustrating though they can be to politicians of both left and right, checks and balances have to be in place if any democracy is to survive. Remove them from the system, as will always be a key objective of the far right, and there is little to stop a strong leader from taking over and outlawing opposition altogether. Autocracy then swiftly follows.

It is chastening, therefore, to note how much of an impact this doctrine is making in the political realm at present. Republican presidential campaigns involving Trump have relied heavily on this tactic, and there is no doubt that it undermines democratic principles by demonising one's opponents, turning them into enemies rather than equal, and supposedly respected, participants in a political process designed to foster diversity of opinion. That kind of generosity is not a characteristic of the far-right mentality, which is more likely to display, at best, a thinly veiled contempt for any who counter it. Bullying and insults are the mainstays of their political discourse, patriarchy at its crudest. It does little for one's faith in human nature to observe the deliberate cultivation of personality cults in such settings, aware of how these can so easily get out of hand, as the history of fascism reveals only too clearly. As Galileo remarks in Bertolt Brecht's *Life of Galileo*, 'Unhappy the land where heroes are needed', and it could be added that unhappier yet is the land that needs a strong leader saviour, who is not to be recommended as a fellow-traveller under any circumstances whatsoever.[10] They are never going to retire gracefully, or leave a legacy of anything but bigotry and prejudice. Generally speaking it will require a revolution to remove them from power (with Bashar al-Assad in Syria the latest to suffer this fate in December, 2024, fleeing to Russia in disgrace).

Authoritarianism never does resolve anything, it merely serves to entrench some of the most unattractive traits of human nature; traits that we should be constantly subjecting to scrutiny, such as abdicating our free will to those in power and going along with whatever they choose to do with this. The only ones to benefit from authoritarianism are those in control of it, yet there are those who entirely approve of that state of affairs and want to impose it on humanity on a permanent basis. There is the famous (or notorious, depending on how you look at it) case of Thomas Hobbes, who in his book *Leviathan* argued that ceding our personal sovereignty to an absolute ruler was the most effective way to prevent civil war. Human beings just could not be trusted otherwise, being driven by their survival instinct to keep amassing greater personal power, so giving up that right was in society's best interests, achieving greater security for all. The power imbalance this inevitably leads to is made quite explicit by Hobbes: 'nothing the Sovereign Representative can doe to a Subject, on what pretence soever, can properly be called Injustice, or Injury: because every Subject is Author of every act the Sovereign doth'.[11] That is authoritarianism taken to its limit, all power residing in the ruler with no safeguards at all for their subjects, and it is the kind of worldview that the far right can always be relied on to support, absolutism ticking all the right boxes for them. It should be seen, however, as yet another misuse of narrative in what is becoming a burgeoning catalogue on the political scene. The rest of us, however, would soon resent finding ourselves being marginalised and silenced by that authority's heavy-handed policing of our actions—the very opposite of what liberal democracy is about. The individual is left with no role to play in this political project but to do as they are told: no objections or protests permitted.

Hobbes can be excused to some extent for the severity of his recommendations because he was working in a time of significant social breakdown, the Civil War period of English history which ended in the downfall of the monarchy in 1649, followed by the execution of the king and the establishment of a republic. This was a case of absurdity writ large in Hobbes's view, therefore demanding the severe measures he went on to propound. Sartre, however, shows us how it is possible to resist such authoritarian impulses even in extreme conditions like these; absurdity cannot be policed out of existence. A Hobbesian state is a far less attractive prospect than one based on existentialist principles; the fact that it would appeal to Autocracy, Inc. is all the more reason to make sure it stays in the realm of fiction only.

Gray's Pessimism

John Gray's pessimism is of a different order entirely to the 'positive' I am recommending we adopt, as his *The New Leviathans: Thoughts After Liberalism* makes clear. In Gray's reading, it is liberalism that is to blame for our current political ills, because of its insistence that democracy was the answer to the whole world's problems. In his reading, however, that is a mere delusion: 'there is no reason to expect one mode of government to displace all others. ... The world of the future will be like that of the past, with disparate regimes interacting with one another in a condition of global anarchy'.[12] It is the Hobbesian message updated: effectively a state of nature internationally, where there are enemies everywhere and security is permanently at risk. Gray's addition to the message is that it is pointless trying to change this condition for the better (even Hobbes had a solution, distinctly unappealing though it was). In this study's terms of reference that would equate to giving in to nausea, which is precisely what I am arguing we should be resisting as strongly as we can—while acknowledging the pull it can exert on us emotionally in the desperate geopolitical condition we are currently mired in. While I would agree with Gray about the gravity of the situation and the difficulty of dealing with the conflicting forces lying behind it, I would not see that as a reason for abandoning liberalism. Unless you accept that there is an inevitability to the fate that Gray posits for us, then it is always worthwhile trying to extend liberalism's influence and offering an alternative to the authoritarian imperative.

I would want to emphasise the social-democratic side of liberal democracy in this proposed alternative, but as argued before, there is a spectrum of opinion to be taken into account there, from left to right, the crux being that it is all firmly anti-authoritarian in outlook. Unless all of the latter is kept going, and kept developing to be able to respond positively to new situations as they arise, with the parties involved debating with each other all the time and open to negotiating compromises to prevent conflict, then the future will not be so much like the past as far worse than it. That would mean there would be little opposition to the likes of Autocracy Inc. Socialists like myself are going to be much more bothered by the threat of the latter than by liberalism; you can argue with a liberal, you cannot with a committed authoritarian, whose reflex reaction is to prevent arguments with them from taking place at all. Free speech is a one-way system to the latter: it is what they decide it is, and only what they decide it is, and increasingly it is the case that they are in control of the means of disseminating it too. Social media platforms can be bought and manipulated to the owner's wish, as various recent examples, such as X, demonstrate only too ominously.

We are far more likely to be plunged into global anarchy by the far right than woke liberals, therefore, as the former would regard such an outcome as an excellent pretext for setting about imposing their authoritarian control over the mass of the population. The more disorder there is (and the far right is very good at fomenting this, being attuned to violent public protests which quickly draw the headlines, keeping them firmly in the public eye), then the more support there likely will be for severe measures to ensure law and order. And 'law and order' solutions of that kind almost invariably involve political repression sooner or later—to the extent of being transnational as well. Whoever causes it, a breakdown in public order tends to be a win-win situation for the far right. The scope for bad faith is substantial in such cases, and the far right will exploit this to the best of its ability (as the riots referred to in Chap. 2 indicate). Liberalism becomes just a pretext for the authoritarian elite to suppress any political views other than those of their self-interested, anti-democratic own. It is also worth remembering that at least some of the disparate regimes mentioned by Gray will not be content with maintaining the status quo, and instead will be striving to extend their power as far as they can. In which case we might well end up with the equivalent of one mode of government internationally, and that will be a range of regimes all on the far right. While these might possibly collaborate with each other up to a point to prevent any resistance against them from gaining momentum, as Applebaum suggests is the pattern now with Autocracy Inc., they would be highly likely to turn on each other if that threat dissipated appreciably: Hobbes's worst-case state of nature, where trust in others has evaporated and it is everyone for themselves. Some form of liberalism has to be kept in play as an option to any such bleak development.

Accepting Gray's premise is ceding far too much scope for action to the far right, which will not be willing to leave any competing liberal polity in peace. Global autocracy would be the more likely outcome to that scenario, with diversity banished from the agenda. Neither is liberalism as imperialist in its aims as the far right will always be, nor as intolerant as many of the world's major monotheisms still are. Both religion and right-wing politics can survive quite easily under a liberal regime, which can encompass different ideological outlooks in a way that authoritarianism will never be prepared to. However one defines liberalism, it is worth preserving as a bulwark against the unmistakably imperialist ambitions of the far right. Apart from anything else, liberal democracy allows governments to change, across the spectrum from left to right, whereas a far-right regime wants to remove that possibility from political life altogether. There is at least some choice in liberal democracy, but none at all under the far right if they are permitted to entrench themselves, as they will always endeavour to do, the one-party state being their standard model.

For Gray, however, there are no such redeeming features to be found in liberalism, which he airily dismisses:

> The current generation of liberals never tires of denouncing the West as the most destructive force in history – racist, imperialist and sexist … Yet these same liberals insist that Western values – human rights, personal autonomy and the like – must be projected to the last corners of the Earth.[13]

Gray makes liberalism sound like a universal theory (which he needs it to be to make his argument work), but it could only be defined as such in the most limited of senses. For one thing its characteristics are much more varied than is to be found in the authoritarian ethos, or than Gray acknowledges (I should emphasise that I do not include either libertarianism or neoliberal economic theory in my own conception of liberalism, as these are largely the preserve of the far right). Faced with a choice between respect for human rights and the obsessive control of an authoritarian regime, one would assume there would not be many amongst the population at large who would willingly opt for the latter. Liberalism can, after all, be modified from within and change over time in terms of its priorities (liberalism now is a very different notion than it was in the nineteenth century, for example). Far-right authoritarianism on the other hand will never feel the need to do this, its overriding concern being to maintain its power by subjugating those it rules to the strictest degree it can achieve. Whether it always gets it right or not, liberalism nevertheless has an abiding sense of the greater public good—not a thought that would ever pass through an autocrat's mind. It will listen to critics in a way that dictators and totalitarian leaders just will not.

Liberalism becomes an all-purpose whipping boy for Gray, but that is to credit it with more power, as well as far greater deviousness, than it actually involves. His critique of it is only too likely to provide more support for the politics of prejudice, which will be quite happy to load all the blame for our social problems on to something as amorphous as Liberalism Inc. Finding someone to blame is a major preoccupation of the far right, and it is never someone of their own ideological persuasion. Blaming is so much easier than trying to resolve social or political problems constructively oneself. As a solution to the critical dynamic between the individual and the collective that liberalism is so concerned to find a balance for, this fails comprehensively. To fall back on scapegoating is to reveal the weakness of your ideology.

Liberalism is, moreover, very much up against it in a world increasingly dominated by social media, which are turning out to be the curse of the age in their ability to spread false narratives and inflammatory rhetoric against vulnerable communities (neither is it just disinformation that social media are spreading; their carbon footprint is massive and steadily growing too, as tracked by groups such as The Carbon Literacy Project[14]). Blaming comes standard with such material, which preys on human weakness in a despicable way that is proving very hard to legislate effectively against. Liberals find themselves forced on to the defensive against the conspiracy onslaught that we are going through, where it is becoming more and more difficult to know what is a true narrative and what is not. It is the latter sort that seem to be swamping the information channels these days, and it is malicious campaigns such as these, not the actions of either liberals or the woke, that is generating global anarchy (global bigotry too). Liberals demand hard evidence for the claims that are made online, evidence that can be verified by several reputable sources, such as those still to be found in the world of traditional news media of both a left and right orientation. The far right do not—except in the echo-chamber of dubious online sites citing only each other as proof, which conspiracy theory is heavily dependent upon (breaking one of the most fundamental rules of philosophy by the practice). That is where the problem really lies for a post-truth age. (It is worth pointing out too that scapegoating the woke has turned into a boring reflex amongst the far right, and adds nothing useful to any debate. Wokeness needs to be reclaimed for the public good, which it was first designed to be; a mental attitude that it is to society's benefit for its citizens to cultivate and keep expressing in engagement with others. It is based on respect for others and a commitment to protecting everyone's civil rights. A full-scale defence of it is long overdue as an antidote to the blaming culture promoted by the far right, where respect for others plays very little part. Not all of us feel that 'human rights, personal autonomy and the like' can be consigned to history as outmoded and then forgotten about.)

Gray is particularly scathing when it comes to the topic of wokeness, which for him is a sign of hyper-liberalism: 'a hyperbolic version of the liberalism the West professed during its brief period of seeming hegemony after the Cold War'.[15] Even if it were as widespread a movement as Gray claims it is, and I am not convinced it is (he can make it sound like some massive conspiracy that has been misleading us as to its imperialist intentions for some time now), one has to ask again, is this really to be feared more than the machinations of the far right and the authoritarian regimes they so much admire internationally? Are human rights such a suspect entity as Gray seems to believe they are, responsible for so many of our problems? To blame liberalism and wokeness for the current state of world politics is to let patently evil actors such as the massed ranks of the far right, plus their distinctive brand of death-threat politics, off the hook. Wokeness does not put people in prison for refusing to follow its dictates: Autocracy Inc. most certainly does, and has no qualms whatsoever about pursuing this policy ruthlessly. While there are aspects of liberalism that can be called into question, it is stretching a point to hold it responsible for anything you do not happen to like about the state of the world around you. The far right has far more to answer for in that respect than liberal democracy ever could.

Gray's argument is notably short on suggestions as to what can be done to prevent a collapse into global anarchy, delivering instead the most conservative of messages that we just have to accept that human nature works that way. It is good to be able to report, therefore, that there are still thinkers around who are trying to find practical solutions to the many crises that mark out the current political landscape, such as the Common Sense Policy Group's *Act Now* project. Although it is specifically addressing British politics in calling for a new Beveridge Report as the basis for an updated social contract, it has implications for any democratic system, not least in its belief that things can be changed from within a polity with the benefit of all its citizens in mind: 'We need to understand that the transformation of society requires systematic democratic reform. ... The reforms call for bravery among politicians in upholding the public good against opportunities for corruption and the power of unsustainable special interests'.[16] Such a firmly common sense-based approach could help to keep populism at bay, reducing the opportunity for bigotry to find an audience. Whether in its liberal- or social-form, it is also an idea that could only come from, and work within, a democracy, where everyone has a stake, and a say, in its outcome. The small-state solution favoured by the far right just leaves the mass of citizens adrift, with little protection when things go wrong or misfortune (in health or economic downturns, for example) strikes. Gray would no doubt regard it as yet another misguided attempt to extend the dominion of Western values, but to a sizeable majority amongst the electorate that would constitute one of its strongest selling points. Whether there is the political will to put their proposals into practice is of course the critical issue in turbulent times such as these, but the motivation behind the project cannot be faulted by anyone committed to democratic ideals. There is such a thing as the public good (it seems bizarre to feel it is necessary to make such a claim), and it can be improved upon if governments put their mind to it. Except, that is, for autocratic governments on the far right: the only thing they want to improve is the extent of the power they hold over the public. Wherever they can be blocked from doing that, then they should be.

Against such democratically inspired initiatives as the *Act Now* group, however, there is the far-right response of America's Project 2025 from the Heritage Foundation think tank to consider. Giving the impression that it has been inspired by the depiction of the Republic of Gilead in Margaret Atwood's *The Handmaid's Tale* as much as anything, the Project recommends a deeply conservative, biblically based approach to both politics and family life.[17] It is anti-diversity, as the far right always is, and advocates a very much smaller state than exists anywhere in the West at present, to the extent of closing down most of the major governmental agencies, claiming this would make American citizens more free (yet another dubious use of the word 'free' I would argue). It is also pro-fossil fuels, again a far-right favourite. Whether the incoming Trump regime plans to pick up on any of the Project's ideas is as yet unknown (although it would certainly be in agreement as regards fossil fuels, as Trump's mantra of 'drill, baby, drill' unmistakably signals), but they are consistent with the direction of thought in the current Republican Party. As far as democracy goes, this is a case of bad faith run riot, and it would be no exaggeration to say that much of the world waits in fear to see how this will all play out.

Being Pessimistic/Being Positive

'Things are bad! Things are very bad' indeed, and that is reason enough to feel pessimistic I have to concede. Yet to allow things to overwhelm us to the point of nausea is in effect to give in to the far right, who are working away tirelessly to achieve precisely that objective. Nausea is a sign of our weakness, but we can work against it. By means of a positive pessimism, for example, which would encourage us to keep plugging away at organising opposition and dissent to political authoritarianism and climate change scepticism. We have to keep reminding ourselves that there is still an audience for this, and for continuing to point out as well the unwarranted assumptions and contradictions of universal theories and uncritical belief, in whatever field they are active. None of these ideological positions are consonant with the notion of democracy, which even with its many flaws and considerable room for improvement (as almost any democrat will agree, hence the call for a new Beveridge Report), is still infinitely preferable to being controlled by Autocracy, Inc. and their anti-woke ilk. The 'world after liberalism' sounds a distinctly unattractive place to be, but liberal attitudes will not simply disappear just because autocrats make them difficult to express or live by.

The style of pessimism I am suggesting is far more realistic than the rather nihilistic one exhibited by such as Gray (with all the baggage that any Hobbesian-style solution to correcting our political problems would bring, and that is not particularly attractive to contemplate either), a project specifically concerned to counteract bigotry and the politics of prejudice. It is, as I have been arguing throughout, an existential choice which anyone of a liberal- or social-democratic disposition should feel duty bound to make, because the far right is not going to give up its determined, bad faith-fuelled, campaign of disruption of the public realm. If things are very bad now, then we need to keep reminding ourselves that they could get even worse if we do not keep exercising that choice and resisting authoritarianism in all its forms. Gray cannot be allowed to be the last word on liberalism, nor Hobbes a reliable guide as to how to plan for the political future: Sartre just has to be a better choice. The concept of human rights can be abused, but that does not mean it is intrinsically wrong-headed or against humanity's best interests. While it may need to be worked on, it is worth the effort from liberals and socialists alike, otherwise waiting authoritarians will gladly step into the breach and that will be the end of human rights: how that would make things better for society at large has to be a mystery to me, but we know who it would benefit and how they would abuse the power it would give them. This has been, as titled, a somewhat despairing conclusion on human weakness (a state of mind it is difficult to avoid as an existentialist, I would argue), but nothing like as despairing as that offered by Gray and the anti-woke brigade.

Living with Nausea Now

'Things are bad! Things are very bad: I've got it, that filthy thing, the Nausea'.[18] That was where we started, with nausea pictured as an insistent threat because of a complex series of socio-political developments combining to put democratic ideals at risk internationally. In effect, something of a perfect storm in terms of the liberal democratic enterprise, with assorted authoritarians, climate change sceptics (plus their many powerful corporate backers), and conspiracists all lining up to trash Western values and the political system built on these. It constitutes a large-scale, entirely premeditated, and deeply anti-social campaign of bad faith, offering a desperate vision of the future, and that is why we (meaning anyone not on the far right of the political spectrum) should be actively campaigning against it. Existentialism encourages us to meet bad faith with authentic behaviour, where our actions are based on a realistic assessment of the situation we find ourselves caught up in. That means making choices that respect the dynamic between the individual and the collective, rather than adopting the world-weary response of a neoconservative like Gray, who haughtily assumes our individual choices will have little impact on how society develops in the longer term anyway. Hobbes or Sartre? Those of a liberal disposition will have no difficulty in making that particular choice. An existentialist worldview would seem to me to be precisely what our current circumstances call for, enabling us to identify and then resist the lure of bad faith—and as it is bad faith that is largely responsible for the problems we are confronted by in public life at present, then that alone proves just how relevant a thinker Sartre is to us now.

Ultimately, what existentialism is telling us is that, even in the most straitened of circumstances, there are always choices we can make. They may not be the ones we would prefer to have, in fact only too frequently they will be anything but, but they do exist and we have at least that much control over our future (allowing for this to be curtailed to a degree when something as extreme as torture is involved). The politics of prejudice want to narrow down the choices available to us quite drastically, but we do not have to go along with their tactics, such as their championship of the strong leader ethic, or of conspiracy theories with no rational evidence at all to back them up, or universal theories which depend on uncritical belief in whatever the authorities say. None of these can be said to be in the wider public interest. The most basic sovereignty we have is at the level of individual choice, and if we give that up, as the far right, channelling Hobbes amidst an unfortunately well-established modern tradition of demagogues, would like us to, only they will gain from it not us individually. Existentialism is a philosophy for hard times and we are most definitely in those again now. Nausea is its low point for the individual, but it can be overcome, as long as we refuse to accept the solutions (pseudo-solutions as I would define them) that the far right are always trying to engineer around us. Overcome, yes, but never completely excised from our emotions; existentialism is not going to pretend otherwise. We have to be permanently on our guard against the possibility of worst-case scenarios coming to pass, and given that there are more than enough of these on the geopolitical horizon to keep us occupied for the foreseeable future (Albert Camus's *The Myth of Sisyphus* has to come to mind, particularly in the wake of Trump's re-election[19]), Sartre has to remain a highly valuable fellow-traveller.

Notes

1. Jean-Paul Sartre, *The Reprieve* (1945), trans. Eric Sutton, London: Penguin, 1986.
2. John Gray, *The New Leviathans: Thoughts After Liberalism*, London: Allen Lane, 2023.
3. Jean-Paul Sartre, *Being and Nothingness: An Essay on Phenomenological Ontology* (1943), trans. Hazel E. Barnes, London: Methuen, 1969, p. 524.
4. Iddo Landau, 'Sartre's Absolute Freedom in *Being and Nothingness*: the Problems Persist', *Philosophy Today*, Winter 2012, pp. 463–73.
5. See, for example, Hannah Arendt, *The Origins of Totalitarianism* (1951), London: Penguin, 2017, and Hannah Arendt, *Eichmann in Jerusalem: A Report on the Banality of Evil* (1963), London: Penguin, 1994. Arendt draws on a range of other authoritative works on the Nazis in her work, particularly in *Eichmann in Jerusalem*.
6. Jean-François Lyotard, *Heidegger and "the jews"* (1988), trans. Andreas Michel and Mark Roberts, Minneapolis, MN, University of Minnesota Press, 1990.
7. See Immanuel Kant, *Critique of Judgment* (1790), trans. James Creed Meredith, Oxford: Clarendon Press, 1952.
8. See Thomas Lewton, 'Inside the Event Horizon', *New Scientist*, 15 June 2024, pp. 32–5.
9. See Anne Applebaum, *Autocracy, Inc.*, New York and London: Allen Lane, 2024, p. 109–112 for a discussion of this phenomenon and some examples of its perpetrators.
10. Bertolt Brecht, *Life of Galileo* (1938), eds. John Willett and Ralph Manheim, trans. John Willett, in Bertolt Brecht, *The Collected Plays*, IV, London: Eyre Methuen, 1980, p. 98.
11. Thomas Hobbes, *Leviathan, or, The Matter, Forme, and Power of a Free Common-wealth Ecclesiasticall and Civill* (1651), ed. C. B. Macpherson, Harmondsworth: Penguin, 1968, p. 265.
12. Gray, *The New Leviathans*, p. 23.
13. Ibid., p. 71.
14. See carbonliteracy.com for details. TikTok appears to be the current worst offender of the major platforms.
15. Gray, *The New Leviatha*ns, p. 114.

16. Common Sense Policy Group, *Act Now: A Vision for a Better Future and a New Social Contract*, Manchester: Manchester University Press, 2024, p. 205.
17. Margaret Atwood, *The Handmaid's Tale* (1985), London: Vintage, 2017.
18. Jean-Paul Sartre, *Nausea* (1938), trans. Robert Baldick, Harmondsworth: Penguin, 1965, p. 32.
19. Albert Camus, *The Myth of Sisyphus* (1942), trans. Justin O'Brien, Harmondsworth: Penguin, 1975.

References

Applebaum, Anne, *Autocracy Inc.*, New York and London: Allen Lane, 2024.
Arendt, Hannah, *The Origins of Totalitarianism* (1951), London: Penguin, 2017.
———. *Eichmann in Jerusalem: A Report on the Banality of Evil* (1963), London: Penguin, 1994.
Atwood, Margaret, *The Handmaid's Tale* (1985), London: Vintage, 2017.
Brecht, Bertolt, *Life of Galileo* (1938), eds. John Willett and Ralph Manheim, trans. John Willett, in Bertolt Brecht, *The Collected Plays*, IV, London: Eyre Methuen, 1980.
Camus, Albert, *The Myth of Sisyphus* (1942), trans. Justin O'Brien, Harmondsworth: Penguin, 1975.
Carbon Literacy Project, carbonliteracy.com (accessed 16 December, 2024).
Common Sense Policy Group, *Act Now: A Vision for a Better Future and a New Social Contract*, Manchester: Manchester University Press, 2024.
Gray, John, *The New Leviathans: Thoughts After Liberalism*, London: Allen Lane, 2023.
Hobbes, Thomas, *Leviathan, or, The Matter, Forme, and Power of a Free Commonwealth Ecclesiasticall and Civill* (1651), ed. C. B. Macpherson, Harmondsworth: Penguin, 1968.
Kant, Immanuel, *Critique of Judgment* (1790), trans. James Creed Meredith, Oxford: Clarendon Press, 1952.
Landau, Iddo, 'Sartre's Absolute Freedom in *Being and Nothingness*: the Problems Persist', *Philosophy Today*, Winter 2012, pp. 463–73.
Lewton, Thomas, 'Inside the Event Horizon', *New Scientist*, 15 June 2024, pp. 32–5.
Lyotard, Jean-François, *Heidegger and "the jews"* (1988), trans. Andreas Michel and Mark Roberts, Minneapolis, MN, University of Minnesota Press, 1990.
Sartre, Jean-Paul, *Nausea* (1938), trans. Robert Baldick, Harmondsworth: Penguin, 1965.
———. *Being and Nothingness: An Essay on Phenomenological Ontology* (1943), trans. Hazel E. Barnes, London: Methuen, 1969.
———. *The Reprieve* (1945), trans. Eric Sutton, London: Penguin, 1986.

Index[1]

A
Absurdity, 3, 6, 21, 22, 59, 76
Adorno, Theodor W., 63, 64
Ally, Matthew C., 4, 14, 40, 47
Alternative facts, 32, 34, 56
Antarctic, 9
Anthropocene, 4, 39, 40
Anti-semitism, 32
Applebaum, Anne, 6, 20, 27, 78
Arctic, 9, 41, 43
Arendt, Hannah, 57, 72, 85n5
Aronson, Ronald, 4
Artificial Intelligence (AI), 10, 34
al-Assad, Bashar, 75
Atwood, Margaret, 82
Authenticity, 3, 10, 14, 25, 38, 40, 41, 50, 55, 56, 70, 72
Authoritarianism, 2–4, 7, 8, 19–35, 37, 47, 57, 60, 71, 72, 74, 75, 78, 79, 82, 83
Autocracy, 8, 64, 65, 74, 78

B
Bad faith, 3, 7, 9, 10, 14, 21, 28–33, 35, 37, 38, 40–44, 46–48, 53, 54, 56–60, 62, 63, 70–73, 77, 82, 84
Bakewell, Sarah, 2, 14, 55
Barrow, John D., 61
Barthes, Roland, 47
Black holes, 23, 73
Boria, Damon, 49
Brecht, Bertolt, 75
Brexit, 6
Butler, Michael, 49
Butterfield, Elizabeth, 48

C
Camus, Albert, 60, 85
Capitalism, 4, 6, 27, 28, 30, 40, 55, 64
Carbon Literacy Project, 79

---

[1] Note: Page numbers followed by 'n' refer to notes.

Caute, David, 10
Chaos theory, 40, 70
Civil rights, 4, 25, 80
Climate crisis, 4, 7, 9, 35, 37–50, 71
Cold War, 5, 8, 80
Common Sense Policy Group, 81
Communism, 5, 12, 22, 25, 55–58, 64
Conservative Party, 29, 45
Conspiracy theory, 3, 4, 6, 10, 36n11, 36n13, 38, 43, 56, 64, 73, 80, 84
Consumerism, 48, 49
COP conference, 40
Copernicus Climate Change Service, 6
Covid pandemic, 6, 29, 31
Creationism, 62
Culture war, 27

D
Dark energy, 61
Dark matter, 61
Degrowth, 42
Democracy, 4, 8, 9, 12–14, 20–22, 25–30, 33, 35, 42, 49, 54, 72, 74, 76–78, 81, 82
Denialism, 27, 56, 60, 73
Derrida, Jacques, 32
Determinism, 3, 10, 63
Disinformation, 20, 24, 59, 79
Dogmatism, 54

E
Engels, Friedrich, 57, 62

F
Fake news, 32, 34, 56
Fascism, 2, 5, 62, 70, 72–76
Fossil fuels, 6, 9, 35, 38–42, 45, 48, 82
Foucault, Michel, 55, 63

Franco, General, 8
Fundamentalism, 54

G
Galileo, 60, 75
Gaza, 6, 23
Grand Unified Theory (GUT), 60–62
Gray, John, 11, 60, 71, 76–84
Great depression, 5
Green energy, 41, 42
Greens, 39
Gyllenhammer, Paul, 40, 46, 47

H
Hate speech, 28
Hegel, G. W. F., 64
Heidegger, Martin, 3, 59, 73
Heritage Foundation, 82
Hitler, Adolf, 8, 22–24, 32, 74
Hobbes, Thomas, 11, 12, 75, 76, 78, 83, 84
Holocaust, 5, 73
Humanism, 60
Husserl, Edmund, 3

I
Immigrants, 31, 32, 34, 36n11, 73
Intergovernmental Panel on Climate Change (IPCC), 38, 43
Irwin, William, 55

J
Jenrick, Robert, 4

K
Kant, Immanuel, 73

L

Laclau, Ernesto, 63
Latouche, Serge, 42
Liberalism, 8, 76–83
Libertarianism, 12, 55, 79
Lovelock, James, 43, 49
Lynas, Mark, 43
Lyotard, Jean-François, 2, 22, 55, 63, 64, 73

M

MAGA, 35, 70
Mars, 7, 40, 71
Marx, Karl, 2, 32, 55, 62, 64
Marxism, 3, 10, 54, 55, 57, 62–65
Middle East, 22, 24, 54, 70
Monotheism, 58, 60, 74, 78
Moos, Markus, 40, 44, 46
Mouffe, Chantal, 63
Musk, Elon, 7, 28
Mussolini, Benito, 8, 22, 23, 32, 34, 74

N

Narratology, 33
Nazism, 5, 32, 33
Nothingness, 59, 73

P

Pascal, Blaise, 2, 59
Patriarchy, 75
Pessimism, 11–13, 44, 71, 76–83
Phenomenology, 3
Populism, 27, 81
Post-Marxism, 62, 63
Postmodernism, 10, 55

Poststructuralism, 10, 55
Project 2025, 82
Propp, Vladimir, 33
Protestants, 58
Protocols of the Elders of Zion, 32
Putin, Vladimir, 6, 20, 21, 25, 30, 34, 59, 74

R

Republican Party, 20, 26, 82

S

Sartre, Jean-Paul, 2–14, 22, 24, 28, 29, 31, 34, 35, 47, 54, 55, 57–58, 63, 70–73, 76, 83–85
  Being and Nothingness, 3, 71
  Critique of Dialectical Reason, 54, 55
  Iron in the Soul, 24
  Les Temps Modernes, 3
  Nausea, 1–3, 5, 7, 22–25, 34, 70
  The Reprieve, 24, 70
  What is Literature?, 54, 57
Scepticism, 9, 11, 35, 57, 82
Shell Oil, 40
Socialism, 55
Social media, 11, 26, 28, 38, 56, 59, 64, 77, 79
Spinney, Laura, 9
Stalin, Joseph, 12
Strong leader, 22, 23, 38, 55, 60, 73–75, 84

T

Tipping points, 9, 22, 38, 70
Totalitarianism, 5, 22, 24, 27, 57, 74

Trump, Donald, 6, 8, 12, 26, 27, 30–35, 36n11, 40, 59, 70, 74, 75, 82, 85

U
Ukraine, 6, 20, 21, 23, 24, 34, 59
United Nations, 42
Universal theories, 7, 10, 11, 27, 53–65, 79, 82, 84

W
Weinersmith, Kelly and Zach, 7
Woke, 2, 77, 80
World War I, 64
World War II, 5, 24, 64, 72, 73

Z
Zuckerberg, Mark, 28